Hope you like the book!

Emmy

PRAISE FOR *Emmy's Question*

"The powerful story of a young girl's struggle with parental alcoholism and the caring adults in her life who made a real difference. A must read for children of all ages."

—Jerry Moe, National Director of
Children's Services, Betty Ford Center

"This is a a remarkable book which provides the reader with an authentic, touching story of a child whose world is turned upside-down due to her alcohol-dependent mother. The subject is presented with sensitivity and understanding, as well as a sincere respect for each of the characters. The author's perceptive use of language makes this an approachable, engaging book, especially for upper-elementary students and would be appropriate for individual or small group reading and discussion. Great books stay in our hearts and leave us better for having read them. This book can be counted among those."

—Mary Ballinger,
5th Grade Elementary Teacher

continued

"*Emmy's Question* is a gift from the heart of a child that connects us to our own losses, and opens a new road ahead. For Emmy, telling her story was the first step toward healing. Stories from the heart, as exemplified in this book, have the power to help us all find meaning and promise."

—Diane Rooks, author of *Spinning Gold out of Straw: How Stories Heal*

"This book is incredibly powerful in its depiction of a young girl growing up with an alcohol addicted mother and the effect addiction has upon the family unit. The distress the child experiences is palpable. Any child who lives in a family with addiction would greatly benefit from this book. An equally important audience is the entire family unit, especially addicted parents, so they may gain insight into the consequences their behavior and choices have upon their loved ones."

—Joan Simon, Psy.D.

"This captivating book should become required reading for children of alcoholics and their families, for it is a message of hope. It is an inspiring story of a young girl's growth and maturity as she realizes that even though she can not fix her mother, she is able to find the best about herself."

—Christy Paul, LMHC

Emmy's Question

JEANNINE AUTH

Morningtide Press
St. Augustine, FL

Published by:
Morningtide Press
P.O. Box 312
St. Augustine, FL 32085-0312
morningtide@bellsouth.net
www.morningtidepress.com

Morningtide Press is pleased to offer a discount to organizations who
purchase this book in quantity. For information, visit our website at
www.morningtidepress.com or call toll-free at 1-877-823-9978

Cover design by Alison Auth
Interior design by Bookwrights
Illustrations by Barbara Acosta

Cataloging in Publication Data
Auth, Jeannine.
Emmy's question / Jeannine Auth – 1st. ed.
    176 p., 19 cm.
ISBN-13: 9780979039522
1. Alcoholism – Juvenile Fiction 2. Children of alcoholics – Juvenile Fiction. 3. Loss
(Psychology) – Juvenile Fiction. 4. Family problems – Fiction 5. Mothers and daughters
– Juvenile Fiction 6. Substance abuse – Juvenile Fiction. I. Title
PZ231.A98Em 2007
813.54 — dc22   Library of Congress Control Number: 2007902282

To Mama and Marsee,
whose love still reaches across time

"I am not afraid of storms,

for I am learning how to sail my ship."

–Louisa May Alcott

Chapter 1

MS. ELLIS WASN'T HAPPY WITH ME TODAY, but I couldn't help it. I was so sleepy my eyes kept crossing and I had to put my head down on my desk. So, guess what? She kept me in at recess.

"I'm worried about you, Emmy," she said. "Is something wrong at home?"

"No ma'am," I said. "There's nothing wrong."

I don't want her or anybody else to know. Grannie says it's okay if I don't want to talk about what's going on. But she also says it's bad to keep everything bottled up inside. So I write in my diary to keep from busting wide open.

Except when I'm doing that, I like to pretend we're just a normal kind of family. You know—like everybody else. But believe me, it's getting harder and harder.

Daddy found out that Mom's been sending me to Tommy's house in the afternoons so she can take a nap. He's real upset. Tommy's mother told him something bad about Mom and says she's sorry, but Tommy can't come over to my house anymore unless my dad is home.

They had an awful fight about it last night. I piled the pillows over my head to try and stop their voices from getting in my head, but it didn't work. They were screaming so loud at each other it felt like my bedroom walls were shaking.

"How do you think it made me feel to find out what you've been doing?" Daddy shouted.

"She's crazy," Mom hollered. "She just doesn't like me. Thinks her precious little Tommy is too good for us."

Daddy yelled something back, but I was desperately humming a song to myself to drown out their hateful words. I thought maybe if I lay real still and didn't move or blink my eyes, the fighting would stop.

Next thing I knew, the clock alarm said time to get up for school.

Ms. Ellis called me down in class again today because I was daydreaming. "What's the matter with you, child?" she said. "Where's your mind?"

My mind was picturing Mom and Daddy and me all holding hands, walking our dog, Raisin. We were joking and laughing together like we were so happy. Like other families. Maybe if I imagine it enough—really fix the picture in my mind—it will come true.

@

When I got home from school, the kitchen was a mess and smelled like burnt tomatoes. Mom had been trying to cook spaghetti. She had sauce spilled all over the stove and splattered on the floor. She kept walking right through it.

"Mom," I said, "don't you see that stuff on the floor?"

"Oh, yeah," she said, giggling, "hand me a paper towel."

She took a few swipes at the floor, then said, "Come here, Baby. I need a hug." When I put my arms around her waist, it smelled like she'd poured a bottle of perfume on herself.

Mom and I have this little game we play. It's called Best Friends Promise. We touch fingers together and she says, "Best friends?" I say, "Best friends, forever."

But really, I just want her to be my mom. If I was actually her best friend, I'd know how to help her and I don't. That makes me feel kind of scared to think she needs me to take care of her. I think it's supposed to be the other way around. And even worse, I think there IS something bad wrong with Mom.

My friend Justina and me were going to play dress-up the other day. We were digging through my old toy chest to get some stuff. We both saw it at the same time. A tall green bottle.

"Ooohhh," Justina said, grabbing it before I could get to it, "what's this bottle doing in your toy chest, Emmy?"

I snatched it away from her and felt my face turn hot with embarrassment. "That's a bottle Tommy and me use when we play Captain Hook and the pirates," I said. I made up some crazy story about Tommy and how he acted just like a real pirate to try and take Justina's mind off the bottle. After she went home, I took it outside and threw it in the bushes while Mom was watching TV.

@

It's happened again. Mom's lost another job. She told Daddy and me it's all the manager's fault. The lady was always picking on her for some reason and just looking for an excuse to fire her. I think it's terrible how mean some people can be.

Mom's had a lot of hard luck lately. She used to be a restaurant manager, but now she's working as a server. She says she doesn't care that she's not the boss anymore because she makes a lot of tips. I'd rather be a boss. That way, nobody could tell you what to do.

I'm never going to get married because husbands and wives try to tell each other what to do all the time.

"I don't understand how you could lose three jobs in a row, Susan," Daddy said to Mom. "It's mighty funny you say it's never your fault." He looked like he didn't believe her. "It better not be what I think it is."

"That's the kind of support I get from you," she said, starting to cry. "I can't help it if people don't like me." Mom picked up a little wooden elephant and threw it at him, then ran to the bedroom and slammed the door.

Daddy started cooking dinner, and I waited for Mom to come back out. She didn't, so I tried to go in the bedroom and make her feel better but the door was locked. I knocked and called, "Mom? Mom?" She didn't answer.

@

Daddy sat on the edge of my bed waiting to tuck me in. Mom still hadn't come out of her bedroom. "Don't worry, Honey," he said. "Everything's going to be okay."

I rolled over and turned my back to him, pretending I was going to sleep. I didn't want to talk to him. He shouldn't have hurt Mom's feelings like that. How would he like it if he'd just lost his job and she acted like it was his fault? She can't help it if people are mean to her.

@

Daddy had to go to work extra early this morning. When I woke up, Mom was still in bed and I was late for school. She didn't want to get up because she had a bad headache. All my clean clothes were wadded up and wrinkled in the dryer, but I pulled out the best looking shorts and shirt I could find and got dressed. Then I couldn't find anything to eat in the house for breakfast except a cup of chocolate pudding. It sure didn't fill me up.

School started off horrible. Some boy I didn't know started teasing me when we passed each other in the hall.

"Hey, girl!" he said, pointing at me. "Don't you own an iron? You're the most wrinkliest kid in fifth grade."

Everybody around us laughed, but I just kept going and acted like I didn't hear him.

Then I had to go without eating because Mom didn't have anything to pack for my snack and forgot to give me any lunch money. Besides being hungry, the worst thing was having old stuck-up Lisa Banks ask me, "How come you don't have anything to eat?"

"I didn't want anything," I said. "We ate a humongous breakfast." I hoped she didn't hear my stomach growling.

❦

Grannie picked me up from school that afternoon. Mom was supposed to be job-hunting. But when we got to the house, she was in bed. Grannie peeked in the room and said, "Are you sick, Susan?"

"I think I have the flu," Mom said, sounding like she had her face in the pillow. "I had a terrible night."

Grannie winked at me and said, "Let's clean up this place a little bit, Emmy. You pick up your toys and other stuff that needs to be put away. While you're straightening up, I'll start doing laundry, and then I'll fix some dinner for you all."

She grinned at me like we had a big secret. "We'll surprise your mom and dad."

Grannie was in a real good mood while we were working. She likes things clean and organized. She washed and dried several loads of clothes from the big basket, and she'd bring them to me to help fold. We were having fun.

"I'm going to go ahead and wash this second basketful that has all these throw rugs and old baby blankets of yours stacked in it," she said. "They smell musty."

I reached in to help her, and there rolled up in one of my baby blankets was a green bottle just like the one in my toy chest. Grannie's face changed for just a minute, then she put her arm around my shoulder and walked me out of the laundry room.

"Precious, let's you and I go see if the potatoes are done, okay?"

Once Daddy got home, Grannie talked to him for a few minutes on the front porch. Then we had dinner, but Mom didn't come to the table. She said she was still sick. Daddy looked like a thundercloud that was getting ready to rain any minute.

"I think you better take Emmy to spend the night at your house tonight," Daddy said to Grannie.

I love to go to Grannie and Poppy's house, but I didn't want to leave. "No, Daddy," I said. "Mom needs me to take care of her."

"You go and have fun," he said, handing me my pajama bag. "I don't want you worrying."

For some reason, it made me want to cry when he said that, but I didn't. If I let myself cry, it's like admitting something is really wrong.

Chapter 2

TODAY TURNED OUT BAD, TOO. A girl named Christi is my new friend. Her mother called my mom and invited us to have lunch at McDonald's and go to a movie with them. Mom was excited about meeting her, but started acting funny before it was time to go.

It took forever for her to get ready. She changed clothes a thousand times and kept putting on more and more make-up. Then she drowned herself in perfume again.

We were late. She stumbled and almost fell going into McDonald's. Then she got into an argument with one of the workers about the toy in my Kid's Meal. It was so embarrassing because she was fussing real loud about it. "It's okay, Mom," I said. "I don't care what they give me. Please don't say anymore."

Then she knocked her cup of water over, and went to get another one. When she tried to sit back down in her chair, she missed and fell on the floor.

Christi's mother helped me pull her up. She made sure Mom was alright. Then she said, "Susan, I'm so sorry, but I have a terrible headache. I'm afraid we can't go to the movie after all."

On the way home, Mom said she thought Christi's mother was a snob. I think she's a very nice lady myself, but I could tell she didn't like my mom. It makes me sad because I'd been hoping Mom would make a nice friend. I don't like any of her friends except Aunt Beverly, and she doesn't come around a lot anymore.

@

I think Mom's in big trouble. My teacher Ms. Ellis called Daddy at work. She told him that Christi's mother called her about what happened at McDonald's. He asked me to tell him about it, but I wouldn't tell him how awful it was. I know there's something wrong with Mom, but it would make me feel really bad to talk about her. Even to Daddy.

I saw Christi on the playground at school, but she wouldn't play with me. "Your mother's weird," she said.

"She is not," I said. "If you say that again, I'll beat you up."

I grit my teeth hard to keep from crying. Mom says I'm

her special angel that God sent to make her happy. If I'm her special angel, I have to protect her, right? So I did what I had to do.

But now Christi's not my friend anymore.

◉

The next day when Grannie and Poppy took me home, we found Daddy emptying bottles of wine into the sink.

"What are you doing, Jack?" Grannie said. "What's wrong?"

"This is what's wrong," he said, pointing to the different-colored bottles lined up on the counter. "Susan ran into the back of a boat trailer this morning. The deputy gave her a DUI, and I had to put her car in the shop. While I was cleaning it out, I found four bottles hidden in the trunk and two under the seat."

He held onto one of the pink bottles so hard I could see his knuckles turn white. "This has been the problem all along."

"What's a DUI, Daddy?" I said.

He sighed as he put his arms around me and squeezed. "It means your mother had been drinking too much wine, and it caused her to have an accident."

My heart did a somersault. "Is she in the hospital?"

"No, Sweetie," he said. "She's over at your Aunt Beverly's. And we need to talk."

◉

Grannie and Daddy and I sat down at the kitchen table for our talk. He asked me to look him in the eye.

"Emmy, you need to know something," he said, taking hold of my hand. "Your mother is sick."

I was about to throw up. "Is she going to die?"

"No," he told me, "she has a disease called alcoholism. There are places that operate like a hospital where people can get treatment for it. I've found a very nice one where she can get help."

I yanked my hand away. "I don't want her to go away."

"I know," he said. "I don't like it either, but we have to get her well."

Right then, I hated my daddy. How could he send my mom away?

@

It was still dark outside when I felt Mom slip under the covers and pull me close to her, just like she used to do when I was little.

"Hey, Mommie," I whispered with a smile, snuggling under her arm and into her warmth. Then I realized she was crying. "Are you okay?"

"No, Baby, I'm not," she said against my ear. "I don't want to have to leave you."

"Then don't."

"I have to," she said. "Your daddy's told you about my problem."

"If you loved me, you wouldn't go."

"Oh, Emmy, you know I love you," she said, hugging me even tighter.

"How much?"

"More than anything in the whole wide world."

"Then it's easy," I said. "Just stay here and never ever drink any more wine."

"No, Baby, its not easy," she said, her breath hot against the back of my neck.

❦

I miss Mom so much. She's been gone for weeks and weeks and weeks now. I wish I could talk to a friend about it, but I don't want anyone to know. Nobody, nobody, nobody could understand the way this feels. If I couldn't write in my diary, I'd probably explode. And if I didn't have old Dolly to talk to, I'd be the loneliest person in the world. I squeeze her so hard at night, it's a wonder all her stuffing doesn't come out.

My stomach hurts all the time. Maybe I'm going to die. Maybe I deserve to die. Maybe I caused Mom to be sick and have to drink because I wouldn't mind her. I was supposed to be her angel and make her happy, but I couldn't. How was I supposed to do that?

Chapter 3

*H*OORAY! MOM'S COMING HOME TODAY! Daddy says she's all better, and we're going to be like a brand new family.

I'm going to be the best kid that ever was. I'm going to clean my room and make good grades and tell her a thousand times every day how much I love her.

Things are going good. Mom's not the same since she got home. We eat our meals on time now, and she's trying to keep the house clean. And I don't hear her and Daddy fighting anymore. Yea!

She's going to meetings every morning called Alcoholics Anonymous or AA for short. It's for people just like her who aren't supposed to be drinking. I don't know what they do there besides talk, but she says they help each other.

Daddy's going to a meeting called AlaNon. He says it helps to talk about my mom's drinking and our problems. Why in the world he wants to do that—I can't figure.

I don't want anybody to know. I'm too ashamed. Kids don't want to play with you if they think your mother's weird. Christi sure won't play with me anymore since that day at McDonald's. Neither do any of her friends. I think she must have told them—that's why.

Mom and I had a great talk today, though. "Oh, Baby, I'm so sorry for what I put you through," she said. "Things are going to be different. I promise I'll never take another drink." We did our Best Friends Finger Promise, and I could tell she meant it this time. I am SOOOOOOOOOO happy!!!!

@

Mom has a new job. Daddy's not sure he likes the idea because she's going to be working at night. He also doesn't like it because it's at a fancy new restaurant where they serve alcohol.

"You shouldn't be anywhere near the stuff, Susan," he said. "The temptation's just too great."

"Oh, you worry too much," she said. "I'll be making really good tips and we need the money." She put her arms around his neck. "I promise. I'll never go back to the way I was. And it won't be long before I'll be a manager again."

My heart lifted like a butterfly when I heard her say that. Now I can stop worrying. She really, really means it.

⊚

I can't believe it! For my tenth birthday, Grannie signed me up for dancing lessons. I get to take ballet and tap and wear cool-looking black leotards and pink tights. We'll be performing on stage, too. What I really like is the girls in my class are so nice. Maybe I'll make a new best friend.

Ever since Mom had to go away to the clinic, Justina's mother says no every time we ask if she can spend the night. Daddy says that parents worry when they know that your mother is an alcoholic. He needs to tell Justina's mother that Mom doesn't drink anymore.

⊚

Well, guess what? Mom is a liar. A big, fat liar! Daddy had to get me out of bed last night to go looking for her. She was supposed to get off work around midnight, but didn't come home. Daddy was afraid something bad had happened to her. He even called the Sheriff. We looked in the parking lot of the restaurant and everywhere he could think of. But we couldn't find her. I was scared to death she'd been kidnapped.

But you know what? She finally came home, and she was *DRUNK!* When I saw her like that, my insides felt like they were shriveling up into a hard little ball.

And Daddy was so mad! The crazy thing was that she didn't think she'd done anything wrong. She was actually mad at him because he'd been out looking for her. Said he was spying on her. They had a terrible fight, and yelled so loud the neighbors probably thought they were killing each other.

I'm embarrassed to walk outside the house this morning. I don't want to go to school, either. I've been wide awake most of the night, and I don't feel like pretending I'm happy. How can you be happy if you can't trust your mom?

Chapter 4

$\mathcal{H}$ERE WE GO AGAIN! Mom got fired. She swears she didn't do anything wrong, just like last time. "I'm the best worker they've got," she told Daddy. "It's not my fault if there's a couple of trouble-makers who have it in for me. They were jealous because they heard I was being moved up to management."

"Get serious, Susan," he said. "You're drinking on the job. I talked with your manager."

"He's a liar," she said. "Don't you think I know better than to do that?"

This time I don't believe her. I know she's lying to Daddy about not drinking because ever since that night she stayed out so late I spy on her. She goes over to Tom and Annie's next door and they sit out back and drink beer. It makes me want to scream and holler and throw rocks at them.

Maybe I should tell Daddy, but I don't want him to be any madder at Mom than he already is.

@

My head hurts so bad. I'm having headaches almost every day now. Dr. Hopkins did some tests and says I'm okay, but I don't feel okay. When I told my teacher Ms. Ellis that I needed to go to the office and get medicine for my headache again, she hugged me and said, "Don't worry so much, Emmy, everything's going to be all right."

I think she must know about my mom. I'm so ashamed, I can't even look her in the eye.

@

Ever since Mom lost her job, she spends most of the day in bed. She called Grannie this morning and told another super-duper lie. "Can you come pick up Emmy and take care of her today since Jack's working?" she said. "I'm sick again, and there's no food in the house. I had to fix the child a rootbeer float for breakfast."

She fixed me a rootbeer float, alright, but we had plenty of cereal and milk. She just wanted Grannie to feel sorry for me so she'd come get me. That way Mom could go back to bed and drink and smoke cigarettes. I know that's what she's doing.

When I get home from school, the place is a mess. And she's got that sticky sweet smell again when I hug her hello. It makes me want to up-chuck.

I try to straighten the house a little before Daddy gets home so he won't know what Mom's doing. It scares me to hear them fighting. If I could only find out where she's hiding her bottles, she wouldn't be able to drink anymore.

The whole time I was at Grannie's, I had a headache. That's because she kept talking about how awful Mom looked and how worried she was about her. "She's too thin, and her color looks bad," she said. "Something's going on."

Grannie has a way of looking at you like she can see right into your mind. "Is there something you need to tell me, Emmy?"

My head was pounding like a tom-tom. Maybe if I told, she could get Mom to stop. But if I did tell on her and Mom found out, she might think I wasn't really her best friend. She might even think I don't love her, but I do. I really do.

"My head hurts too bad to talk, Grannie," I said.

@

The most horrible thing ever has happened. Mom's gone, and I guess I'm to blame. I finally told on her. But the reason I did is because I'm afraid she's going to die if she keeps doing what she's doing. Every day she's been getting worse. I'm afraid to ride with her when she takes me to school because she acts like a nervous wreck. Her hands shake like an old lady's, and she talks crazy sometimes.

Daddy's been working long hours at work and is under a lot of stress, so I'm worried about him, too. I didn't want to make it any worse for him by telling. But when I caught her pulling a bottle of wine out from under her mattress right before we were supposed to leave for school, I knew I had to do something.

"What's that, Mom?" I said.

She jumped like a scared rabbit and tried to hide the bottle in her arms. "Oh, it's just my new medicine. I hid it because I don't want your Daddy to know about it. He's worried enough about me as it is."

She looked right at me and lied. My own mom.

"I know what that is, Mom. It's wine. And I'm going to tell Daddy."

She started trembling all over and grabbed my hand. "No, Baby, don't do that, please. Your daddy's the reason I'm drinking. It's all his fault to begin with, and he'll take you away from me."

Her eyes were red and watery. "You don't want that to happen, do you?"

"No!" I said, feeling scared. I couldn't imagine not being with my mom. "But you won't stop drinking."

"I promise I will, Baby," she said, grabbing my hand. "I'll go to my AA meeting this morning right after I drop you off at school. I promise—if you just won't tell your daddy. Give me another chance, please." She was begging.

My stomach was doing flip-flops. "Okay, if you really mean it," I said, "let's do the Best Friends Promise."

She gave me a quick hug, and then, right there, we did our Promise. "Okay, Mom," I said. "I'm believing you. No more drinking, right?"

"No more drinking, Baby."

But then that afternoon, Mom picked me up from school. The minute I got in the car, I knew she was drunk. And she had some woman with her who was drunk, too. It was disgusting. Not only was I mad, but I was scared. She kept running the car off the edge of the road, and they were squealing like it was fun.

She pulled into the parking lot of a liquor store, and they both jumped out. "Mom, what about me?"

"We'll just be a minute," she said, giggling with the woman as they walked away.

How do you think I felt sitting in front of a liquor store? Stupid and ashamed! And besides that, some of the men coming in and out of the liquor store were scary-looking. When Mom and her friend didn't come out after awhile, I finally hunched down on the floorboard of the car so no one could see me.

So that's why I told Daddy. As soon as he got home. Everything! He was hopping mad, and right away went out to her car and found a couple more bottles. When he came back in, he looked like a tornado tearing through the house. I ran to my room and quick-like closed my door because I didn't want to hear what was coming. It didn't work, though. They both started off screaming at the top of their voices.

"How *DARE* you do this, Susan, after what we've been through? Think about what you're doing to your daughter. And see this bill? Nine thousand dollars to send you to rehab, and what good did it do?"

"Oh, shut up!" Mom said. "All you think about is money, money, money. I don't have to listen to anything you say. The truth is, if I didn't have to live around here, I wouldn't need to drink."

"Sure," Daddy said, "always try to blame it on someone else. That's your problem. You won't ever accept any responsibility, will you?"

"That's a joke," she shouted. "I'm sick of responsibility! I'm getting out of this place. You or nobody else is ever going to tell me what to do again."

I heard Daddy say something else, but I couldn't understand him. Then the door suddenly slammed.

By the time I got to my window, Mom was already backing out of the driveway.

Chapter 5

SO MANY THINGS ARE SWIRLING around in my brain, my head feels like a Tilt-a-Whirl. Mom's been gone a week now, and I think it's all because of me. Well, maybe Daddy, too, but mostly me. I'm the one who tattled on her. And I keep remembering what she said in that fight with Daddy.

"If I didn't have to live around here, I wouldn't need to drink," she said.

She must have meant that living with me and Daddy makes her drink. Maybe it IS my fault. I try hard to be good and mind her, but I know lots of times I act like a brat. Maybe that's the real reason she left.

At first, we didn't know where she was. Then Daddy found out she was staying with the so-called friend who went to the liquor store with her. He told Grannie and Poppy that she's on a binge, whatever that means.

@

My dance recital is tomorrow. I can hardly wait. Dancing is one place where I can forget about things. Nobody knows about Mom, and I can just be like everybody else. I even have a new best friend. Her name is Camilla. She's really neat and wears pink glasses. Her mother is very, very nice, and said yes when Camilla asked if I could spend the night after the recital. I couldn't believe it.

I'm trying not to let myself be sad about Mom not being there. My aunts and uncles are coming, along with Daddy and Grannie and Poppy. If anybody asks me why my mother isn't there, I'll just tell them she's sick. And that's the truth.

@

Yesterday at the recital was the worst day of my life instead of the best. At first, everything was going great. Grannie came backstage to help me get dressed for my ballet and tap numbers. Our costumes made us all look a lot older and sophisticated, particularly with our makeup on. When it came time for us to dance, I was hardly nervous at all. I love being on stage, and I only forgot one step.

Afterwards, all the parents rush down front to the dancers and give them flowers. I was standing there looking for Daddy in the crowd when I heard Mom's voice calling above all the noise.

"Emmy, Emmy! Here I am, Baby! Here I am!"

I couldn't believe she'd remembered my recital, even though she'd been gone. I was so excited. Then I got a good look at her, and so did my friends. She was waving her arms around like a crazy person. Her face was all puffy and red, and her hair was in clumps. I guess she cut it herself. She kept bumping into people left and right as she wobbled down the aisle.

Camilla and her mom were standing next to me. "Is that your mother?" Camilla said.

I could have died. "Yes," I said. "She's been sick."

Mom grabbed me and hugged me so hard, we both almost toppled over. I was really happy to finally see her, but I knew she'd been drinking bad. She could hardly even pronounce her words.

"Aren't you glad to see me, Baby?" she said.

"Of course, Mom," I said, which was the truth. Even the way she looked. But I sure didn't want my friends to see her like that.

Afterwards, when Grannie had helped me pack up my costumes and it was time to leave, I figured Camilla's mother would say it would be best if I didn't spend the night. But thank goodness, she acted like nothing had happened. I tried to act that way, too—wearing my happy face.

I had a terrible dream at Camilla's house last night. I woke up screaming at the top of my lungs, and it about scared Camilla and her mother to pieces. She called my daddy. I tried not to cry in front of them because I didn't want them to think I was a baby. But as soon as I saw Daddy when he came to get me, I couldn't hold it in any longer. I blubbered.

He almost smothered me, hugging me. "What's the matter, Honey?" he said. "What'd you dream?"

"You and me and Mom and Raisin were at home, all together again," I said, clinging to him. "We looked out the window and saw a huge black tornado coming towards us. We screamed to Mom to run—that it was going to hit us." I couldn't stop crying, telling him about it.

He squeezed me and kissed the top of my head. "Well, Princess, that was just a nightmare. You don't have to—"

"No, Daddy. It was like it was real," I said, pulling away from him. "We kept begging her to come with us, but she just stood there not paying any attention to us while the tornado began tearing our house apart. The walls started crashing in, and we screamed and screamed, but she wouldn't move."

I could hardly say the next part. "It killed her, Daddy. It killed her."

He picked me right up in his arms and held me close, just like he used to do when I was a teeny baby. "Don't you worry, Sweetheart," he said. "Everything's going to be all right. We'll get Mom to listen. Don't you worry."

Chapter 6

J DON'T KNOW HOW DADDY DID IT, but he got Mom to come home. Everything's not okay, though. She's still drinking, and Daddy and me both know it. Not only can you tell by the way she acts, but this time, she admits it. If Daddy says anything to her about it, she cries and says she has to have it—that nobody understands what it's like. She just picks at her food and is getting skinnier and skinnier. I don't think he knows what to do about it. Neither do I.

It's so scary. It's like she's here with me, but she's not. She doesn't even seem to notice or care about my headaches. I tell her that when she smokes cigarettes, it makes my head hurt worse, particularly in the car. But she goes ahead and does it anyway. Parents aren't supposed to do that, are they?

Grannie took me to the grocery store with her today. We were going down the frozen food aisle, and I happened to look across at the other side. I'd never noticed it before, but the whole aisle from one end to the other is all wine bottles. Suddenly, I started bawling, right there in the store.

"Why are they selling that stuff, Grannie? It's killing Mom." People were looking at me, but I couldn't help myself. "Please tell them to stop selling it, Grannie—please!" I was really wound up—wailing. "It's not right, it's just not right."

"Blow your nose, Honey," she said, handing me a handkerchief, "and let's finish up here. We need to talk, okay?"

As soon as we got in the car, I said, "I'm so sorry, Grannie, for making everybody look at us. I don't know what's the matter with me."

"I do," she said. "You're frightened, and you've been trying to hold it all in. That's the worst thing you can do. And you need to understand that it is legal to sell alcohol. Not everyone has the problem with it that your mother has, thank heavens. It doesn't affect them the way it does her because they're not alcoholics."

She began looking through her pocketbook for her car keys. "What you need to do right now is to learn everything you can about alcoholism and how to cope with your feelings."

"What's cope mean?" I said.

"It's an important word that means learning to deal with your problems. We all have to do it sooner or later." She looked at me over the rim of her sunglasses and said, "Remember, I asked you if you wanted to go to AlaNon? Although it's for grownups, I could call and find out if some of the parents bring their kids with them. They may have some kind of opportunity for you to share, also."

"No, I can't talk to anybody else about it. I'm too ashamed."

"That's the first thing that's going to have to change," she said, shaking her head. "You don't have anything to be ashamed about. You have no control over your mother."

"Maybe not, but I'm not going," I said. I was about to throw up, just thinking about it.

"Well then, we're going to try something else," she said, starting the car.

No telling what Grannie had in mind, I thought, staring out the window as we pulled out of the parking lot. She was pretty stubborn, and when she had her mind made up, you better watch out.

@

The next thing I knew, Grannie had made an appointment for me with a counselor.

"Why'd you do it, Grannie?" I said, really upset with her. She made me so mad sometimes. "The other kids will make fun of me if they find out I had to see a counselor. They'll think I'm strange."

"Oh, Honey, that's silly," she said.

"No, Grannie, really. I saw a movie once on TV about this messed-up bad kid whose parents took him to a psychologist. They didn't know what else to do with him. The boy was seriously scary, but the psychologist was even scarier."

"Well, believe me," she said, looking pleased with herself, "the person you'll be seeing is not at all scary. I know you're going to love her."

Yeah, right, I thought.

Chapter 7

I DIDN'T FINISH ANY OF MY WORK in school today. All I could think about was my appointment with the counselor. Grannie told me when I got there, I needed to open up and talk about my feelings. Anything I wanted to say. Even though I felt like my head might pop open with all the thoughts I have bouncing around in my brain, how could I talk bad about my mom? Especially to a stranger? I told Grannie there's things I can't even tell her.

"That's exactly why I made the appointment with a counselor for you," she said. "Ms. Carol is a very, very smart lady who can help you, I'm sure. She's easy to talk to, and works with kids just like you every day."

"I don't think there's anybody else in the whole wide world just like me," I said. "Who else has to worry about their mother all the time?"

"You may be surprised," she said.

Well, Grannie was right. Ms. Carol turned out to be a super nice lady. It wasn't at all like I thought it was going to be. For one thing, she has twinkly eyes that look at you like she's especially interested in what you're saying. Lots of grownups don't care what a kid has to say. But she made me feel important right off the bat.

"The first thing we all have to agree on is that anything Emmy wants to tell me will stay in this room," she said, handing us a paper. It was a form she had me and Daddy and Grannie sign saying we all agreed to that, and then she signed it, too.

She said kids have a right to privacy—just like grownups. I liked the sound of that. It made me feel a lot better, just in case I did decide to talk about Mom and how I was feeling. Not that I was going to, of course.

After Daddy and Grannie left the room, Ms. Carol smiled and said, "Do you like to play games?"

"Sure," I said, thinking that was a strange question for a counselor to ask.

It turned out she had lots of games packed away in a big box. "I love games," she said, pulling one out.

It was Uno, and I'm pretty good at it. We played for the rest of the hour. She didn't ask me questions about Mom like I thought she would, though. We just talked about little stuff.

I don't know whether her boss knows she plays games during work, but it was sure fun. I like Ms. Carol a lot.

⊚

I give up! There's no way I'm ever, ever, ever going back to school. Daddy and I were supposed to meet Mom there for Parents' Night after she got through with her AA meeting. She showed up all right, but the minute she walked in the room, I wanted to run. You could tell she'd been drinking.

Something about alcohol makes her body not work right. She walks like a spider with her legs apart, with her arms held out like she's trying to find something to hold onto. Everybody moved away as she headed straight for me.

The first thing she did was grab me around the waist and drag me up to Ms. Ellis's desk where she and a couple of parents were talking. Mom butted right in.

"I'm Emmy's mother," she announced in a megaphone voice like they should all be impressed. When nobody said anything—just stood there looking at us—she kind of laughed an un-funny laugh and said, "What's the matter? Am I invisible or something?"

I was dying. It was as if everybody in the room stopped perfectly still. Out of the corner of my eye, I could see the other kids staring at us.

Ms. Ellis's face was shiny red. She reached out and took Mom's hand. "Oh, excuse me, dear," she said. "I'm glad to finally meet you. We're talking about the carnival coming up."

Just then Daddy came back from the bathroom and saw what was happening. Mom was mumbling something that didn't even make any sense.

"We've got to go, Susan," he said, touching her elbow. "Thanks for the cookies," he said to Ms. Ellis as he began steering Mom to the door.

"I can walk out of here on my own," she said, jerking away from him and knocking over a desk with a crash as she stumbled ahead of us.

Every eye in the room watched us leave.

Today on the playground was like a bad dream. The kids who used to be my friends stood around in little groups, eyes cut sideways at me, giggling and whispering behind their hands. They all said no when I asked if they wanted to play a game. So I got on the monkeybars by myself and pretended I was having a good time even though my head hurt something terrible.

Afterwards, in the bathroom, I was blinking back tears when Tamara came in. She always likes to play tag with me. "I'm sorry I can't be your friend anymore, Emmy," she said. "My mama says so."

All I could think about when I went back to class was

wondering if Mom had any idea what she was doing to me. Or did she even care? No, that's not right. Of course she cares! I know she loves me. More than anything in the whole wide world, she says. That's what I don't understand.

◎

Ms. Carol listened without saying anything while I told her what happened at Parents' Night. She didn't even have to ask me anything, I just busted out telling her as soon as I sat down. It felt good to be able to talk about it to somebody.

"How did that make you feel?" she said in a quiet voice.

"Awful. Like I wanted to crawl into a crack."

She twirled a pencil on her desk. "Are you mad at your mother?"

"No," I said. "Well, yes—I am, I guess."

"Does that make you feel guilty?"

"Uh-huh," I said, feeling uneasy.

"Why?"

"Because she's my mother, and Daddy says she's sick. So I can't be mad at her."

Ms. Carol wrinkled her brow. "Who says?"

"I don't know. I just figured it, I guess."

Ms. Carol got something out of her desk drawer, then came around and sat in the chair across from me. "Catch," she said, and tossed me a beanbag. "Go ahead, throw it back," she said with a smile.

Once I got over being surprised, we got in the rhythm of tossing and talking, and that's the way I learned it's okay to be mad with Mom.

"You're correct about your mother being sick," Ms. Carol said. "Alcoholism is a disease, but she is still able to make choices. She chooses to drink. Don't you dare feel guilty about being mad. You're having to bear the consequences of her actions, and of course you're angry."

I tossed the beanbag a couple of times before I screwed up the courage to say, "But what if I'm the one who caused her to be sick?"

"What makes you think that?"

"Maybe I don't always behave like I should."

"You and all the other kids in the world," she said with a laugh.

"No, I mean it. I'm not good about things like doing my homework on time and stuff. Maybe it's made her nerves bad. She says she needs to drink so she'll be calm."

"That's because she's addicted to alcohol. That's what addiction is. Her body is telling her she needs it and will feel better if she drinks."

"That's a dirty trick."

"You better believe it. And it's not your fault," she said, holding the beanbag in both hands and looking me square in the eyeballs.

I could tell Ms. Carol knew what she was talking about, and it made me feel so much better I wanted to jump up and kiss her, but I didn't.

Instead, I told her what popped up in my mind. "Even if it's not my fault, Ms. Carol, Mom says I'm her best friend, so I need to find a way to make her stop drinking."

"That's a whole different ballgame, Emmy," she said with a sigh, glancing up at the clock. "Our time is almost up for today, so we'll have to talk about that next time."

Chapter 8

SOME NIGHTS I LIE IN BED and think about when I was little and didn't have any worries. I don't know whether Mom was drinking bad then or not, but she was lots of fun and made me feel special. I had a little blow-up plastic pool, and I remember her filling it with water and she'd get right in it with me. We'd splash and have a great time. She'd play Barbies with me for hours, too, and we'd always do the Best Friends Finger Promise.

I remember a nursery rhyme I used to say sometimes at bedtime with her: *I wish I may, I wish I might, have the wish I wish tonight.*

If I had a Fairy Godmother who said I could have one wish, I know what it would be. I don't need toys or clothes or anything else. I just want my mom to stop drinking. To get well.

Please, God—this is me. If you're listening, make her get well.

◎

I slept late this morning, and the first thing I heard when I opened my eyes was Daddy talking in a low voice to somebody in the living room. Through my window, I saw a car in our driveway with a green map of Florida painted on the side. It looked like some kind of government car. Uh-oh! Something was way wrong. I tiptoed over and smashed my ear against the door so I could hear what they were saying.

Daddy was talking. ". . . take my responsibilities as a father seriously," he said.

"I'm sure you do, Sir," a man's voice said. "But we have no choice other than to follow through when we get these reports. The child's welfare may be at stake."

"That's understandable—you're just doing your job," Daddy said. "I assure you, though, the problem's been over-blown. That was a single incident. Susan's a good mother, and she loves Emmy very much."

"Have no doubt she loves her, Sir," the man said. "We see it every day. But you'd be surprised how often love is not enough."

"Well, it is in this case," Daddy said. "We're going to work our way through this, I promise. You won't have to make this visit again."

"Good enough," said the man. "I'm taking you at your word. You have a good day now, you hear?"

Daddy mumbled something I couldn't make out, then the door closed. I peeked out the window and watched a big man with a briefcase get in his car, then back out the driveway. From what I'd heard, I knew I never wanted to see him again.

@

Daddy was cleaning out the refrigerator when I walked into the kitchen. "Well, good morning, Rip Van Winkle," he said, knuckling the top of my head. "I thought you were going to sleep all day. How about some Rice Krispies?"

"Where's Mom?" I said.

"She's starting a new job today."

"Another one?"

"Another one," he said, reaching for the cereal.

"Who was that man?"

"Just somebody on business."

"What kind of business?"

He pushed the bowl towards me. "Eat your cereal, Emmy. It's nothing for you to be concerned about."

"Daddy, I'm not a baby anymore. Tell me. We're in trouble, aren't we?"

He sighed like it was his last breath, then slumped in the chair across the table from me.

"I wouldn't say we're in trouble, Honey, but your mother's drinking is causing some problems. It's not for you to worry your little head about, though. Its my responsibility. I've got to make her understand this can never happen again."

"Why? What happened? Who was that man?" I said, even though I was afraid to find out.

"This is not something you can talk to your friends about," he said with a no-funny-business look.

"Friends? You think I've got somebody I want to tell THIS to?" Daddy doesn't have a clue sometimes.

"Well, it's just not something we want known," he said, combing his hair with his fingers. "The man was Mr. Anderson from Children's Services."

"What's that?"

"A Florida state agency that makes sure children are being taken care of."

"So? I'm being taken care of. Why'd he come here?"

"I don't know who it was," he said, "but someone at Parents' Night saw your mother's behavior and called and reported it. So Mr. Anderson—"

"Oh, that's just great!" I yelled, feeling my whole body on fire with shame. I could just hear everybody talking about us after we left the room that night. "You think it was Ms. Ellis—or one of the parents?"

"I don't know, Emmy, but it really doesn't matter who did it. It's done."

"Well, it matters to me," I said. "How would you feel

44

when you were a kid if you knew people at school felt sorry for you, and even reported your parents to the police?"

"He wasn't a policeman, Honey," he said, rubbing my arm. "Remember the field trip your class took last year to the courthouse and you got to meet the judge? Well, Mr. Anderson ultimately has to report it to the judge if he finds a bad family situation with children. He had to check out that phone call because lots of parents who drink neglect their kids. I told him over and over that wasn't happening here. Okay?"

When I didn't answer him right away, he tilted my chin up with his finger. "Hey," he said, "are you all right?"

"Does he know about Mom being in the hospital that time?"

"Yes, I told him."

"Does he know about the time Mom left and we didn't know where she was?"

"No. That wouldn't be a good thing to tell," he said, giving me a quick hug. "Don't you worry, Honey. Your mom's starting a new job today, so she should be feeling lots better. Everything's going to work out all right."

I went back to my bedroom so I could think about things. Maybe I was being selfish to worry about what people at school thought about me. It sounded like Mom could be in trouble, no matter what Daddy said. If that man comes back and wants to talk to me, how will I know what is okay to tell him—and what isn't?

Chapter 9

I WANT TO TELL GRANNIE AND POPPY what's going on, but I'm afraid to. Daddy's boss sent him to another town to help open up a new store, and me and Mom have been staying here by ourselves.

Wouldn't you think that since Daddy warned her about the man from Children's Services, she wouldn't take even a teeny sip of wine? But no—she says that makes her want to drink even more. And she is. Lots more. Mom says if I tell on her, Daddy will divorce her. Even worse, she says the state people will take me away from her, or even send her to jail.

She wants us to run away together. It scares me to pieces because I know she's not thinking straight. That stupid wine has her brain all screwed up. If she can't stop drinking here, she'd probably be even worse without our family around. There's no way I want to leave Daddy and Grannie and Poppy, but I might have to, I guess. I'm afraid if I don't go with her, she might leave anyway, and then there wouldn't be anybody to take care of her. I'm afraid she'll die.

How can I let her go off by herself?

Ms. Carol's office always smells like popcorn. Sometimes, she'll hand me a bowl to munch on while we talk.

"So, tell me what's happening," she said, taking a fresh-ly-popped bowl out of her tiny microwave.

Before I even thought about what I was doing, I told her how bad things were. How Mom was drinking all the time, and how she and Daddy were fighting every night even though I hadn't told on her, and how Mom wanted us to run away together so the state people couldn't take me away from her, and how worried I was because I couldn't figure out how to fix it.

"What makes you think you can fix it?" she said, plucking a piece of popcorn out of my bowl.

"I don't know," I said. "If I could at least make Mom stop drinking, she and Dad would stop fighting, probably."

Ms. Carol flipped through a file folder on her desk, then said, "I seem to remember your telling me that you ought to be able to save your mom because you're her best friend."

"That's right—I am," I said, suddenly having to fight back tears. I pretended to be picking at a spot on my jeans. "She's lost her other real friends. Even Aunt Beverly doesn't have anything to do with her anymore."

"Emmy, look at me, " she said softly, leaning across her desk. "Look at me."

She waited, then said, "What you *ARE* is your mother's child—a youngster—and it is not your responsibility. You cannot control your mom's drinking."

"I could do a better job, maybe, of finding her wine bottles and dumping the stuff out."

"It wouldn't matter if you found every bottle that ever came into your house," she said. "As long as your mother wants to drink, she will. Hear me. You did not cause this, and you can't do anything about it."

"But I love her and she loves me and who's going to help her if I don't?"

"You already help her just by loving her," she said. "And so does your daddy and the rest of the family. But an alcoholic needs the help of people who are trained to treat the disease."

"She already went away once to a hospital," I said, "and it didn't do any good."

Ms. Carol closed the file folder and put it in her desk drawer. "Sometimes people aren't ready to accept help."

"But why not?"

"Because their brain is telling them they need the

alcohol to feel normal. Remember we talked last time about what being addicted means?"

Suddenly my head hurt so much I could hardly see. "I've got a bad headache, Ms. Carol."

"It's about time to go anyway, Emmy. Your daddy's waiting outside." She helped me up and put her arm around me. "Come on."

I leaned against her as she was getting ready to open the door. "I don't want my mom to be addicted, Ms. Carol."

"I know you don't, Emmy," she said. "I know you don't."

@

Daddy glanced at me as he pulled out of the parking lot. "Did you have a good session with Ms. Carol?"

"Uh-huh," I said, slumping down in the seat.

"You need to sit up straight in that seat belt, Emmy."

"Okay."

"Something wrong?" he said, looking at me in the rear-view mirror.

"Got a headache."

"Do you need some of your medicine?"

"Don't think so. But it hurts to talk."

"Okay, Honey, then we won't talk," he said. "I'll just drive."

I turned my head and stared out the window as we drove down Main Street. We passed by one of the restaurants where Mom used to work when I was about four. I remember she used to bring me left-over lobster sometimes because it's my favorite. She'd heat up butter for me, and we'd have a race to see who could eat the most lobster the fastest. She was so much fun back then.

Daddy put on the brakes, stopping for a red light. It's the busiest intersection in town. I sat right there looking out the window and counted five more restaurants where Mom had worked, then lost her job. I remembered the stories she'd tell about how it happened—always blaming somebody else for it. I used to believe her, and I'd be really mad at those people.

Now I know it wasn't always somebody else's fault. Thinking about it made the stabbing pain at the back of my head worse.

"Daddy, I do need to take some of my medicine," I said.

@

I had the tornado nightmare again last night. It's always the same. We see it coming, big and black—then we feel it thundering, shaking the ground—and Daddy and I yell at Mom to run, but she ignores us. It tears our house apart, and then I know Mom's gone. She's dead.

Oh, dear God, this is me again, Emmy. If you can hear me, don't let Mom die. If there's something I can do to make you want to help us, let me know, okay?

Chapter 10

WHEN I WALKED INTO THE KITCHEN, Mom was sitting at the table with her head propped in her hands. Her eyes were closed. She didn't move.

I gave her a quick kiss on the cheek, then pulled out the chair next to hers.

"Morning, Mom," I said. "You okay?"

"I'm great," she said.

She didn't look great. Her face was blotchy and her eyes were full of red squiggly veins like she'd been crying a long time. Her hand shook as she reached over and grabbed my arm.

"You know why I'm great, Baby?"

"No, Mom."

"Because today is the first day of the rest of my life,

and I'm not going to take a drink. You hear me, Emmy? I've promised your daddy, and I'm promising you." She swiped at the tears spilling down her face. "I'm not ever going to take another drink. I mean it. Because I can't afford to lose you."

"Mom, you could never lose me," I said, jumping up to hug her. "I would never leave you."

She rested her head against me and said, "I know you wouldn't, Emmy. That's why I've got to do this. I've simply got to."

@

Daddy and I talked all the way to school about Mama's new promise.

"I think she means it this time, don't you, Daddy?"

He grinned at me, then reached over and squeezed my hand hard. "I do, Honey," he said. "I really do. For one thing, she's going to change jobs."

"Don't tell me," I said. "Again?"

"Yes," he said with a quick smile, "but this time it's a restaurant that doesn't serve alcohol, so she won't be tempted working around it. And she doesn't know it, but the manager is an old friend of mine—Teresa Bright—a wonderful woman who mothers everybody. She'll be good for your mom."

"I don't know about that," I said. "When Grannie tries to mother Mom, she doesn't like it, even though she's trying to help her."

"Well, your mother sees that as Grannie trying to tell her what to do," he said, pulling up in front of the school. "Grannie tends to be bossy at times. It'll be different with someone outside the family."

◎

Poppy picked me up from school today. When we walked through the front door of our house I could hardly believe my eyes. Mom actually had everything looking neat and clean. It even smelled clean. I was so proud.

"Looks as if your mother's been busy," Poppy said, squeezing my shoulder.

"Sure does," I said. "You know she's not drinking anymore, don't you?"

"That's what I hear," he said, walking around and checking things out. Poppy's kind of nosy. "It's an answer to prayer, Munchkin, I'll tell you that. Your mom's a good person. She simply needed a reality check about what was wrong with her life. For some alcoholics, that never happens."

"How come?" I said, pouring both of us a glass of orange juice.

"Because it's too easy to blame their unhappiness on something else. They think it's because of their job or their families or their finances—or maybe even their dog. Anything but the alcohol."

"Sounds like Mom," I said. "She kept saying she needed to drink so she could handle all the bad stuff that kept happening to her because of other people. She told me it helped her."

"Well, there you have the most insidious thing about alcoholism. That's what they believe, and it holds them prisoner."

"What's insidious?"

"It's something that doesn't seem as if it would hurt you, but can cause great harm. If you're an alcoholic, you think that glass of wine is your friend, but in actuality it's your poison."

"Oh, Poppy, I'm just so happy Mom finally figured out the truth before it was too late."

"Me, too, Munchkin," he said. "Me, too."

Everything's so good for me lately I could jump for joy—*boinngg, boinngg, boinngg*—right up to the stars. It's like I'm living in a different house. Mom loves her new job, and her boss has promised her that she can get back into management if she shows them she can handle it. She doesn't make as much money as she used to because people don't tip as much in restaurants that don't serve alcohol. Like Daddy says, though—that doesn't matter. What matters is that we're a family again.

Mom's different because she's not drinking, and they're not fighting anymore. I go to bed at night and sleep without any bad dreams. Ms. Ellis is proud of me because I've pulled all my grades up to A's and B's. I'm proud, too. And believe it or not, I choreographed a tap number for the school talent show all by myself. It got lots of applause.

But best of all, Daddy says I can ask Camilla to come next Saturday on his day off for a playdate at my house. I don't have to worry about Mom embarrassing me in front of my friends anymore. I've been so lonely. Can hardly wait.

Chapter 11

MAYBE THIS IS ALL A BAD dream and I'm going to wake up any time now. It just can't be happening. Not when everything was going so good.

Camilla and me had a blast yesterday, and after we begged and begged, her mom said she could spend the night. Daddy fixed barbecue on the grill for us since Mom was working, and then we watched one of my favorite videos. Afterwards, he made us promise we'd go on to sleep because we had to go to Sunday School in the morning.

We talked and giggled for a while, and Camilla told me a funny story about her daddy and their pet rabbit. I remember getting sleepy and thinking how happy I was.

The next thing I knew, I had to go to the bathroom, and I noticed the kitchen light was still on. Daddy was sitting at the table—not doing anything—just sitting there.

"What are you doing, Daddy?" I said, looking at the oven clock. "It's after 2:00 in the morning."

"Waiting on your mom," he said, without moving. My stomach twisted in a knot. "She's not home yet?"

"No."

"Have you heard from her?"

"No, Honey, I haven't."

"Maybe she had to work late."

"Maybe."

I could tell he didn't think so. I was about to say we might better call the police when car lights swung into our driveway. "This must be her," I said, running to the door.

"Wait a minute," he said. "Let me see who it is."

Before he could say anything, a key turned in the lock and in comes Mom and two other women. Drunk. Holding each other up and laughing like fools. My mom. The one who was never going to take another drink. I just stood there, not believing it.

Daddy grabbed her by the arm. "What do you think you're doing, Susan? Get these people out of here!"

"You can't tell me what to do," she said, yanking her arm away from him. She got right up close to his face and said, "This is my house and I'll do what I want."

"No, you won't," he said, "not as long as Emmy and I are living here."

One of the women motioned with a big bottle she was carrying and said, "Oh, come on, Susan. He's a turkey. We'll go to my house."

Daddy wrapped his fingers around Mom's wrist. "You're not going anywhere," he said. "If they don't have a ride, I'll call a taxi for them."

"Get your hands off me," Mom hollered, trying to pull away.

Instead, he tightened his grip on her wrist and she started yelling like a banshee and beating on his head with her other fist.

I couldn't stand it. "Daddy, let go," I said, pulling on his arm. "Please let go."

When he did, she stumbled backwards, then made out like she was laughing, but it was a fake laugh. She had the ugliest look on her face I've ever seen. "Come on girls," she said, "let's get out of here."

The door slammed behind them. We could hear them yelling out in the front yard. The car engine revved up, then they screeched off down the street.

"She never even told me goodbye, Daddy," I said. "She didn't even see me."

"I know, Honey," he said. "I know."

Just then I heard a little noise and looked up at the stair landing. There stood Camilla, looking scared like she was in the wrong place for sure.

@

Daddy let us sleep late in the morning and skip Sunday School. I guess he knew I wouldn't feel like talking to anybody. After Mom left, I could tell Camilla felt sorry for me and that made me feel worse.

"Emmy, don't be ashamed about crying last night," she said. "I'd have been crying, too, if my mother had done what yours just did."

"Please don't tell anybody, okay?"

"Don't worry, I won't," she said. "I promise."

"Not even your mother, okay?"

She wouldn't look at me for a minute, then she said, "I have to tell Mama. It's a rule. She says she needs to know if anything bad happens while I'm at somebody's house."

"But she'll never, ever let you come stay with me again."

"I'm so sorry, Emmy, but I have to do what she says. We can still be friends, though."

"Bet we can't," I said, trying not to think what Camilla's mother would really say when she found out about my mom and her friends.

◎

It's been weeks since the night Mom left. She came and got some clothes and stuff while Daddy was at work and I was at school. I knew right away when she'd been there because all her special skin soaps and creams were gone from the bathroom. It looked bare and empty, the way I feel inside.

She's only called me one time, and I could tell she'd been drinking so I hung up on her. Ms. Carol said it wasn't rude under the circumstances. That I had a right to do it because it actually makes me feel sick to know she's talking to me drunk. I mean, couldn't she stop drinking just long enough to talk to me on the phone?

I keep trying to pretend Mom's just on a trip somewhere, but I know that's not what's happening. Grannie and Poppy were over here last night, so I hid on the stair landing to hear what they were talking about. I heard Daddy tell them he was getting a divorce. He said he used to believe he could control Mom's drinking by staying with her, but realized if she would do what she'd done in front of me, there wasn't any hope. He said I was his first responsibility.

Poppy said there wasn't any question about that, and reminded Daddy about the visit from the man who worked for the State.

"How could I forget it?" Daddy said. "He made it clear I have no choice."

"Good heavens," Grannie said. "I can't believe our family is being dragged into something like this."

Right then on the landing, I prayed that God would look down on Mom wherever she was and zap her hard so she'd understand what she was doing to us.

Chapter 12

MOM'S GONE CRAZY. I heard Daddy tell Grannie that his friend, Teresa, who is Mom's boss, called to report that Mom's been drinking on the job and living with some man she met in a bar. How bad is that? The restaurant gave her a chance to have time off work to go get sober, but she refused. Ms. Teresa said if she doesn't shape up real quick, she's going to have to let her go.

If Mom calls me again, I hope I can tell her how worried I am. How horrible it makes me feel to hear she's hanging out in bars with other men. That's trashy. But it's hard to say things like that to your parent. Particularly when she acts like she doesn't even care.

@

I waited all morning for Mom to show up at Grannie's like she promised. She called just now and told some nutty story about getting two flat tires. This is the second time she's told the same story. I could tell she'd been drinking and was making it up, but I acted like I believed her. I don't know why. I just said, "Okay, Mom. I love you." Why didn't I tell her I knew she was lying? That I'm getting really mad. Why can't I tell her what it feels like?

@

Ms. Carol tossed the beanbag back to me. "So, maybe you ought to try this," she said. "If it's uncomfortable for you to tell your mother you know she's lying to you, why don't you write her a letter? Sometimes it's easier to express yourself that way."

"I already write in my diary almost every day."

"I know," she said, "and that's good. But it may not have the same effect on you as letting her know directly how you feel."

"I don't want to hurt her feelings."

"But you're hurting, aren't you?" she said, putting the beanbag back in her drawer.

I glanced at the clock. Our time was almost up again. It always flies with Ms. Carol. "I'll try," I said. "But it's not easy to tell your mother you know she's a liar."

@

Daddy and I had just gotten home from the PTO Carnival when the doorbell rang. The minute I saw the deputy sheriff standing there, I knew something had happened to Mom. I was about to faint.

"Sorry to be the bearer of bad news," the deputy said to Daddy, "but your wife and a friend have been in an accident. Her injuries are minor and so are his, but the woman driving the other car is in serious condition."

"Was Susan driving?" Daddy said.

"No—her friend was," he said, "but both their alcohol levels were three times the legal limit.

"Were they at fault?" Daddy said.

Before the deputy even answered, I knew what he was going to say. I ran up the stairs, not wanting to hear. I just want it all to go away.

Please, God—please, God—make it go away.

@

The headlines were big and black on the front page of the newspaper: "Pregnant Woman Critical After DUI Crash". There it was for the whole world to see—about how my mom was riding in a car with another man—and they were both under the influence of alcohol—and they ran into an innocent lady who might die. Suddenly, I was so nauseated I had to stop reading and make a run for the bathroom.

I threw up my whole breakfast, and the sour, bitter juice in my mouth burned and made me keep gagging. I was so weak and shaky, I folded into a little ball in front of the commode. The tile floor was cold, but I didn't care. It wouldn't matter if I stayed there all day. At least I wouldn't have to go to school and face the look in Ms. Ellis's eyes. She reads the entire newspaper first thing every morning.

@

It had been over a week since I heard from Mom, but she called me tonight and acted like everything was hunky-dory. She started telling me about her friend, Bob, and how nice he was.

"He loves children," she said, "although he's never had any of his own. He's letting me fix up a bedroom for you so you can come stay."

I heard her take a puff on her cigarette.

"How's that sound, Baby?" she said.

I could hardly breathe. "Is Bob the man you were with when you all had the accident?"

"No," she said, "that's Ernie. He's still in jail. Bob's another friend."

"Where'd you meet him?"

"Oh, he's someone I've known a long time," she said. "A good friend."

I heard her light up another cigarette. "You don't sound very excited," she said. "Your room's going to be really cute.

A girl I work with is loaning me a twin bed that she doesn't need, and I'll try to pick up a pretty bedspread for you. Would you like that?"

I wanted to say, "I don't need a bedspread, Mom. I'm not going to some strange man's house." Instead, I said, "I guess so."

"What's wrong?" she said. "Don't you miss me? Don't you want to come stay with me?"

I felt like saying, "No, I don't. I want you at home with Daddy and me." Instead, I said, "Oh, you know I miss you, Mom."

"I miss you, too—*SO MUCH*. I can hardly wait for you to be here. You know how much I love you, Baby, but I've got to go to work now," she said, sending me kisses over the phone.

I can tell you one thing. It's hard to send kisses back when you're trying to keep from crying.

@

I had to ask Ms. Ellis for permission to go to the office and get my headache medicine again today. When I got back, she asked me to stay in at recess so she could talk to me. My insides curled up when she said that because I knew what it was going to be about.

"I read about your mother's accident in the paper, Emmy," she said, shuffling papers on her desk. She sighed and took off her glasses, then massaged the corners of her eyes like they hurt. "I'm so sorry, Honey," she said, finally looking at me. "I know what you're going through. You see, I'm a child of an alcoholic, too."

"But you're not a child," I said.

"No, I'm not. I'm what is known as an adult child of an alcoholic. That means that although I'm grown, I still remember how hard it was many times to deal with my parents' drinking."

"Both of them?"

"Both of them."

"Wow," I said, wondering how in the world she could stand it.

"What I want you to know, Emmy, is that you can live through these bad times just like I did. You're a smart girl and a good girl. Your mother's poor choices are no reflection on you."

I tried to swallow around the lump in my throat. "But what she's doing makes me feel bad about myself," I said. And then I heard myself asking her what I hadn't even been able to put into words before because it made me feel guilty even thinking it. "What if I turn out just like her?"

"That's a fair question," she said, "and deserves a fair and honest answer. You may have already learned this, but children of alcoholics *ARE* more likely to become alcoholics themselves. That doesn't mean, however, that your future is doomed and that you will follow the same path as your mother.

"I certainly didn't," she said. "I just made up my mind that things would be different for me. My brother, on the other hand, chose to begin drinking when he was about seventeen and he lives a miserable life as an alcoholic today. He's lost almost everything, including his health. It makes me very sad."

"Are your parents still alive?"

"No. They both died years ago. Neither one of them ever stopped drinking." She bent over to put a file in her desk drawer. "You know it's very difficult to quit, don't you, Emmy?"

"Yes, Ma'am. I figured it out. Mom's tried over and over, and now she and Daddy are getting a divorce."

"I heard that they were," she said, nodding her head. "How do you feel about that?"

I looked down at my hand like I'd just discovered a hangnail so she couldn't see the tears stinging my eyes. "Like I'm going to die, Ms. Ellis. I think I'm going to die."

Chapter 13

MOM'S BOSS CALLED DADDY TODAY to let him know she had to let Mom go from her job. I heard him say, "No, I understand, Teresa. You've got a restaurant to run."

They had a long talk. Then he said, "You're right. I'm going to have to talk with my attorney about that."

Later, Grannie and Poppy came over, and I hid on the landing again so I could hear if Daddy told them anything. Which he did. Daddy said that Ms. Teresa knew Mom had been drinking on the job because several customers had complained, but they couldn't figure out where she was getting it. Then they asked to check her purse, and found out she had alcohol in her hairspray bottle.

"That's the sign of a serious alcoholic," Poppy said. "She's in trouble and it's sad, but you need to do whatever you have to do to prevent her from driving with Emmy. She should not be behind the wheel of a car with that child."

"Actually, it's beyond my control, anyway," Daddy said. "Sam Delaney says the judge in all likelihood will not grant unsupervised visitations to Susan because she's already been under the radar of Division of Children's Services. One of us will have to be with her at all times. With the people who are stepping forward with stories about her present lifestyle, Sam says it won't go well for her."

"What people?" Grannie said.

"Both Teresa and another woman who works with her have offered to submit written affidavits to the judge. The other woman used to party with Susan, so she apparently knows a lot about what's been going on for some time. It's not good."

"Not many people care to get involved in a divorce," Grannie said. "Why would they stick their necks out?"

"Teresa says it's because they think Susan's on the skids. They're worried about what might happen to Emmy."

@

I didn't even turn on the lights in my bedroom after quietly closing the door—just found my way in the dark to my bed, felt for Dolly and my old Pooh-Bear and cuddled them close to me, then wrapped the covers as snug as I could around us.

Oh, I want to go back to when I was little and felt

safe. The tornado dream keeps coming back. And now there's a new one where I'm out in space and it's black and I'm falling and falling and there's no one there to catch me. I'm scared in a way I've never been scared before.

I know I've got Daddy and Grannie and Poppy to take care of me. But not Mom, unless I go stay with her at that man's house and there's no way I want to do that. Absolutely no way. It scares me to think that maybe I'll have to.

But the ladies who work with her are going to talk with the judge about it. They said I wasn't safe with her. How awful is it that two ladies I don't even know are worried about me?

Grannie took me to meet Mom today at the Big Chicken. When I caught sight of her standing in the parking lot looking for us, all my anger just washed away and I started squealing like a baby pig. We hugged and hugged and hugged. It was so great, but she feels bony. I don't think she's eating hardly anything.

Grannie carried her book with her and sat in a different part of the restaurant so Mom and I could have some private time together. She said we could have two hours if they didn't need our table.

"Oh, Emmy, I can't look at you enough," Mom said as we pulled out our chairs. "I swear I think you've grown three or four inches already. I've missed you so much."

I wanted to say, "Then why haven't you showed up when you were supposed to?" But I didn't. All that mattered was her sitting across the table from me right then.

"Tell me how things are going at school," she said.

"Okay, I guess."

"Just okay?" she said with a nervous laugh. Her hand trembled as she reached for her water. "What about your friend, Justina? What's she doing these days?"

"I don't know. I don't see her much anymore."

"Really? What about Tommy?" she said, snitching one of my french fries.

"Him, either."

"Oh, well," she said, shrugging her shoulders, "you'll make new friends at Bob's place when I can get you there. I'm working on it with my attorney. I'm sure I saw a girl about your age down the road."

My brain was awhirl trying to think what to say. Finally, I said, "Daddy says I can't go there."

Her eyes glinted. "Oh, he does—does he? Well, we'll see about that. You're my daughter and I'm not giving you up."

A little thrill went through my body even though I was scared about having to go to Bob's place. At least she still wanted me.

Grannie came over to our table and said she was sorry, but it was time to go. Mom put on her sunglasses that are so dark it's like looking into a black hole, and we walked outside. When I turned to hug her goodbye, streaks of wet black mascara were running down her face from under her glasses. She put out her finger. "Best Friends?"

I touched her finger with mine and said, "Best Friends." Then I real-fast squeezed her as hard as I could, jumped in the car, fastened my seatbelt, and began waving goodbye through the window. As Grannie pulled out of the parking lot, I turned around in the seat and looked back.

There she was—standing all alone—still waving.

@

Mom does love me, I know. I'll bet when she finds out the judge won't allow her to drink and be around me, she'll be able to toughen up and say goodbye to drinking wine for good. And she'll come home.

@

From my bedroom window, I watched Daddy and his friend jump into the monster truck crammed full of most of our furniture. It pulled out of the driveway groaning and swaying like it could hardly carry it all. Daddy had said for me to pack the rest of my stuff for the next load while Grannie and Poppy cleaned things downstairs. But I didn't want to.

My bed, my dresser, my chest of drawers, and my old toychest were gone. My room already looked deserted even though the walls were still covered with my posters and pictures. My collection of stuffed animals sat posed and empty-eyed on the shelves.

When Daddy told me we needed to sell the house and move to an apartment, I started bawling.

"Please, Daddy, you can't do that. Don't make us leave—please, Daddy, don't."

"I have no choice, Honey," he said. "I can't afford to keep the house now that your mother's gone. Maybe you'll actually be happier in the apartment complex because I'm sure there will be lots of kids."

"No, I won't be happier," I said, crying harder. "This is my house and I don't want anybody else to live here. What about all our pets that are buried out in the back yard? Elmo and Homer and the fish? Who's going to put flowers on their graves?"

"I'm sorry, Emmy," he said, wrapping his arms around me. I could feel his heart thumping hard. "I'm doing the best I can," he said. "Believe me, I'm doing the best I can."

That made me feel terrible right away because I knew it was true. Daddy has to take me to Grannie and Poppy's house to spend the night now during the week because he goes to work at 4:30 every morning. That way, he can be home to spend time with me after school. It's really hard on him. Not many daddies would do that.

Thinking about our conversation made me feel guilty all over again. So I got busy and started taking the pictures down from the wall. When I came to the big one of me and

Daddy and Mom and Raisin sitting on the front porch, I stared and stared and stared at it. I must have been about four years old, and we looked like the perfect American family. Were we? No. Not at all. My mom must have been drinking even then to be so bad now.

In a flash, before I realized what I was doing, I raised the picture frame over my head and slammed it down on the floor, shattering the glass.

I felt wild and looked around for something else to break. Oh, yes! My old dollhouse, sitting in the corner. When I was small, Mom and I spent many hours playing with it and the make-believe family.

Suddenly, I knew the truth, and even my skin was on fire with fury. Yes, that's what I had all along! Just a make-believe family.

I stood in front of my beautiful dollhouse and slowly and deliberately and with all my might stomped on it—and stomped on it—and stomped on it—until it was splintered to pieces—just like my family—broken to bits.

©

Grannie and Poppy never asked what happened when they saw my dollhouse smashed to smithereens. They never told Daddy, either. Grannie knows I'm having a hard time about things and says I can talk to her or Ms. Carol anytime I want. But mostly we just act as if everything is okay. Mostly I try to forget how mad and hurt I am.

My new bedroom in the apartment Daddy rented is pretty. Grannie took me shopping for a new bedspread, curtains, and rugs. We chose a pink and lavender and green color scheme. She says since I'm staying with them a lot while Daddy is working, I can have my own bedroom at her house, too. She says I now have two homes and to be thinking about how I want to decorate my room.

Maybe I won't need to do that, though. I haven't told anybody, but I'm still hoping Mom and Daddy are going to make up. That we can be a real family again. It may be crazy, but every day I imagine how it's going to be. Just like in the movies.

There's room in the apartment for Mom—no problem. She and Daddy are supposed to go before the judge next week, and I know when the judge gives her a choice of alcohol or me, she'll come back home. She just has to.

Chapter 13

I SCREAMED AND SCREAMED AND SCREAMED like a maniac all the way to Grannie's house after the judge's court hearing—until my head felt like my brain was going to explode and splatter all over the inside of the car.

"HOW COULD MOM CHOOSE ALCOHOL OVER ME??" I shrieked. *"HOW COULD SHE CHOOSE ALCOHOL OVER ME?"*

I kicked and pounded my fists against the seat like some little baby in a helpless tantrum.

"How, Grannie? How could she *DO* it? She says she loves me!"

"Your mom does love you, Emmy," she said, glancing at me in the rear-view mirror, "but she's hit rock bottom and probably realizes she's in no shape to take care of you."

"Then why not just quit instead of giving me up?" I yelled, kicking the back of the seat again and again. "What kind of mother would choose alcohol over her child? I hate her—I hate her—I hate her!"

"Believe me, Angel, this kind of thing happens every day," she said, turning into her driveway. "I know you're broken-hearted. And I know you're angry. I'm angry, too. But I don't think you hate your mom. What you hate is the alcoholism. There is a difference."

❦

I tried to draw a picture today of what I feel like inside, but it's too hard since I can only draw stick-figures. How do you draw mad and sad and ashamed and loving and scared and guilty, all at the same time?

❦

"So now I have a mother that the judge says isn't allowed to drive me anywhere in a car, or even spend any time with me alone," I said, plopping myself down on the little sofa in Ms. Carol's office. "That's just great, isn't it?"

Ms. Carol studied me for a minute, then said, "Do you understand why the judge made that ruling?"

"Yes, Ma'am. It's simple. Because I've got a mother who chose wine over me. Alcohol makes your brain not work right, so he thinks I'm not safe with her. All she had to do was tell the judge she'd quit drinking—but no. Out of all the mothers in the world, I had to get one who likes wine better than her kid."

"It's much more complicated than that, Emmy," she said, handing me her usual bowl of popcorn from the microwave. "But we're not going to talk about your mother today. We're going to talk about you. You're the one who needs help right now."

When she said that, all those things I'd been holding tight inside just let loose and I started blubbering, dripping tears and snot all over my popcorn.

"I know I'm acting like a big baby," I said, wiping my nose on my sleeve.

Ms. Carol handed me a box of tissues. "Go ahead and cry, Emmy. Everybody has feelings that need to—"

"You don't understand," I said, hardly able to get the words out. "I'm so ashamed, I could just die."

"Why are you ashamed?"

"Because I've got a bad mother." By then, I was really wound up and crying all over myself.

Ms. Carol took off her glasses and laid them on the desk with a sigh. "No—you have an addicted mother. Remember, we talked about this before?"

"But what's everybody going to—"

"Are you worried about what other people are going to think? Or are you worried about what Emmy is thinking?"

"Both!" I said, my voice cracking around the lump in my throat.

"I'll tell you what I think," she said, leaning back in her chair.

"What?" I blew my nose with a snort.

"That you have the right to think good things about yourself—and that your feelings are normal. The best way I know for you to believe this is to listen to the kids I told you about in my small group. They can relate to what you're going through because they've been there."

"You mean their mothers left—"

"Not all of them, no. But some have problems with both parents. No two families are identical, Emmy, but you share a common bond. You're not alone in this."

She readjusted her glasses on her nose. "So, what do you say? You want to give it a try?"

I didn't even have to think about it. "Yes, Ma'am," I said. "I'm ready."

At school today, I could hardly keep my mind on my work. Ms. Whittington wrote my name on the board three times and got mad with me because I was not paying attention. I surely do miss Ms. Ellis, my teacher from last year. At least she understood what was wrong with me when I got like this.

During my math test, I couldn't even remember my multiplication tables. All my brain could think about was going to my first meeting with Ms. Carol's group after school.

When the bell rang, I crammed my books and folders into my book bag and made a bee-line to the place where Daddy always picks me up. My heart sunk when I saw Jackie and Abigail and Jamie huddled in a little group there, giggling and having a great time. They were in my class last year and we were friends, but after Mom made her grand appearance at the Parents' Night, they never included me in anything again.

When I see them together like that, it makes me self-conscious because I feel like they're talking about me and my family, making fun of me with their knowing eyes. So I just acted as if I didn't notice them and stood with my back turned, watching for Daddy.

Just as I caught sight of his silver SUV turning the corner, Madison Banks, who is one of the most popular girls at school and always waits in the same place to be picked up, too, sidled over to me.

"Hi, there! I see your daddy coming to pick you up all the time," she said. "I know it's really hard not to have a mother and—"

Daddy pulled up to the curb just then. "Don't be stupid," I said, glaring at her as I opened the car door. "Everybody has a mother, including me." I slammed the door as hard as I could.

Daddy looked over his shoulder and said, "Who stepped on your toes?"

"Oh, that girl made me so mad! She's just another Miss

Priss trying to act superior and make me feel bad about Mom. I'm sick of it."

Chapter 15

WE WERE A FEW MINUTES LATE for Ms. Carol's group meeting because Daddy and I went to the wrong room. By the time we found the right one and he hugged me goodbye at the door, I was so jittery I was about to barf. I didn't know who would be there or how to act. I said a little prayer that they wouldn't think I was a complete idiot—took a deep breath—and walked into the room.

The kids were all seated in a big circle. And guess who I saw sitting there with her big moon eyes—no joke—looking at me? Madison Banks! The girl I'd just called stupid.

Unbelievably, she smiled and waved like she was glad to see me, motioning for me to come sit by her.

This can't be real, I thought as she gave my hand a little squeeze when I sat down. Madison, the awesome basketball player, the star of the last school play, the girl everyone thought was cool. What in the world was *SHE* doing here?

I was so rattled I hardly heard Ms. Carol introducing me to the group.

". . .so we're going to do things a little differently today and not have the regular program", she was saying. "Go around the circle and give your name—then tell a little bit about yourselves if you want to. But right now, I want you all to welcome Emmy."

They all yelled my name and clapped like crazy. As if they were really glad I was there. Then one by one they said their first names. Some of them told a little bit about why they were in the group.

". . .and when they put my daddy in jail, I thought I was to blame for telling on him—what he did," said a cute boy named Joseph. "I felt guilty for what happened."

"Yeah, that was me," said another boy sitting next to him. "My mama used to tell me if I'd behave myself, my daddy wouldn't drink. So every time he'd get drunk and beat her up, I'd think it was my fault—that I must've done something wrong."

"What do you all have to say about that?" Ms. Carol said.

I jumped straight up—spooked—as everybody hollered like they were cheerleaders, *"IT'S NOT YOUR FAULT!"*

Ms. Carol nodded her head and grinned. "That's right, it's not your fault," she said. "You didn't cause the bad things that happen."

Then a girl named Tamara said, "I used to feel so ashamed because my parents made me think we had this deep, dark secret that I should never talk about. You know, about what went on in our house at night."

Another girl joined in, saying, "Yeah. I know what you mean. My mother acted like it was okay that my stepfather beat the daylights out of her every time he got drunk, but she'd warn me not to say anything. When I'd see her with a new black eye or busted lip, it made me feel bad about myself. I figured if she didn't think she was worth much, I must not be worth much, either."

"Anybody want to comment on that?" Ms. Carol said with a raised eyebrow.

A real perky older girl named Susie held up her hand and said, "What I had to do was realize that it was my parents who had the problem; not me. I felt like a loser for a long time because they both were drunk more than they were sober. I didn't start feeling better about myself until I joined this group and discovered I wasn't the only one with a dysfunctional family."

"Right on!" yelled a black boy I'd seen before in the school musical. "There's lots and lots of us! We're all over the place."

Everybody laughed, and I realized I was beginning to relax a little. It was now Madison's turn. I couldn't imagine what she would have to say or why she was even there. Surely, she didn't have an alcoholic in her family!

"I'm Madison, as you all know," she said, "and you've heard this before since I've been coming to group longer than any of you. But I'm going to tell my story again for Emmy."

She turned to face me and said, "First of all, when I asked you that question at school today, I wasn't trying to be nosy or mean. Somebody told me they thought your mother was dead and I—"

"That's not true!" I said, my face hot with embarrassment. "And people shouldn't be talking about me behind my back."

"No, no—it wasn't that way at all," she said. "I'd asked about you because I noticed you standing off by yourself all the time. That's the way I used to be, so I wanted to make friends with you."

"Huh! You weren't ever like me," I said. "You're one of the most popular girls in school."

"Well, I don't know about that," she said with a grin, "but I do have true friends who like me even though my mother's in jail."

"Your *WHAT*??"

"Uh-huh. She was not only a bad alcoholic, but did drugs, too. She was a nurse, and started stealing pills from the hospital where she worked. She got caught."

"Oh, how horrible. I'm so sorry," I said, feeling like a numbskull for calling her stupid. "It's just that when you—"

"That's okay, Emmy, I understand. You're going through what I went through for a while—and just about everybody else in here, too."

"We sure did," the girl named Susie said. "Doesn't matter who you are, it's not any fun being the kid of an alcoholic."

"No, but guess what?" Madison said. "You don't have to give up and feel sorry for yourself and be miserable. There's ways you can learn to be happy, no matter what your parent is doing."

"Couldn't have said it better myself," Ms. Carol said, smiling and ringing a little red bell. "That's all the talk for today, kids. Time for refreshments."

Before I could gather up my things, everybody stampeded for the back of the room except for Madison, who stayed in her seat.

She handed me a little address book. "Why don't you give me your phone number so we can talk?" she said. "You'll see. Everything's going to be okay."

I very carefully wrote my name and phone number in the tiny space, then handed it back to her.

"Great," she said, glancing at it. "Come on, now. Let's go get something to drink."

@

I about talked Daddy's arm off on the way home. That meeting was awesome. Just to know there are other kids like me is great, but to have Madison as a new friend is the BEST. It's better than anything I could dream of. I won't have to be ashamed talking with her about Mom. She understands.

Chapter 16

THE PHONE RANG AND RANG AND RANG before I could turn off the shower and wrap a towel around myself. "Oh, I hope that's Madison," I thought, grabbing for the phone.

"Hi, Baby," said Mom in a scratchy voice. "What're you doing?"

"Taking a shower and waiting for a new friend to call me."

"Really?" she said. "Who's that?"

"Her name's Madison."

"Really?" she said. I could hear her sucking on her cigarette like a fish gulps air. "Where'd you meet her—at school?"

"You might say that," I said, crossing my fingers. It

wasn't a real lie, though, because I had seen Madison at school before I actually met her in Ms. Carol's group. For some reason, I didn't want to tell Mom about going to group or why I had to go.

"Well, what's been going on?" she said.

"Nothing."

"Really?" she said. "What about dancing?"

I heard her puff on her cigarette again and realized how much I hated the sound. Every time she did it, a little picture would come in my brain of poisonous smoke traveling through her lungs, turning them black and shriveled.

"Why do you keep saying 'really?' And another thing is, why don't you stop smoking?" I said, surprised at myself.

She exhaled sharply, whistling through her teeth. "I guess it's just awkward trying to talk to you, that's all. That's why I haven't called you. You're mad with me, aren't you?"

"I just don't want you to die of lung cancer."

"No, Baby, I'm not talking about that. I'm talking about the court hearing. You're mad."

"It's okay," I said. What was wrong with me? It *WASN'T* okay. Mothers don't choose alcohol over their kids. It stunk!

"Well, I promise you I'll make it up to you," she said. "Just as soon as I get back on my feet, I'll have you come live with me and Bob. How would you like that?"

I wanted to tell her there was no way I'd ever live with her boyfriend. Instead, I just said, "You've got to quit drinking, Mom."

I heard the flash of the lighter as she lit up another cigarette.

"Absolutely, Baby, I promise. You'll see. Believe me?"

"Um-hmmm, I said." Yeah, sure. When turtles fly.

@

The more I thought about the conversation with Mom, the more miserable I got. It must have shown on my face because Grannie came out on the porch, took one look at me, and said, "Good heavens, child! You look like you're about to cloud up and rain all over yourself. What's wrong?"

"I just talked to Mom."

"Did she say something to upset you?"

"Not really," I said, "but I'm so mad I feel like I'm going to explode."

"Did you tell her that?"

"No. She asked me if I was mad about what happened in court and I told her it was okay."

Grannie shook her head. "No wonder you feel as if you're coming apart at the seams. Why didn't you tell her the truth?"

"I can't."

"You know what I would do if I were you?" she said. "I'd go in my room and grab my pillow and beat it with my fists as hard as I could. Like Ms. Carol says, you've got a lot of anger that needs to come out, and if you haven't reached the point you can be honest with your mother yet, it'll make you feel a lot better."

I couldn't help but giggle. "You mean that, Grannie?"

"I'm serious as a heart attack," she said.

◎

Guess what? I did what Grannie said. I beat and beat and beat my pillow until I expected to see feathers fly all over the room. By the time my arms got tired, I was feeling great.

◎

When we got together at her house, I don't know who talked the most—me or Madison. She started off telling me about her mother, and I could hardly wait to tell her about mine. There was so much I'd tried to hide for so long.

When I got to the part where Mom started staying out and not coming home at night, Madison wasn't even shocked.

"After my mother lost her job and before they arrested her, there were days on end that we didn't know where she was," she said.

"How did you handle that?"

"Not good. I'd stay awake at night crying and imagining her dead somewhere," she said. "Then when I did go to sleep, I'd have terrible nightmares."

"Me, too," I said. "I dream that a tornado wipes out our house and she gets killed because she won't listen to us. She acts as if she doesn't hear us."

Madison took two grape popsicles out of the freezer and handed me one. "You're worried about her dying, aren't you?"

"Sure, aren't you? About your mother, I mean."

"Not so much anymore. At least now I know I can't prevent it if something bad happens to her. She's the only one who can do that."

I bit the end off my popsicle and thought for a minute. "But she's in jail right now, so you don't have to worry because she can't do anything anyway, even if she wanted to."

"That's true," she said with a funny smile. "And I know this sounds crazy—I never told anybody—but I was actually a little relieved when they put her in jail because I knew I wouldn't have to worry about her doing drugs and drinking for a while."

"No joke?"

"No joke." She started giggling. "You ought to see your tongue, Emmy. It's bright purple. You look like you've got the crud or something."

"Huh!" I said with a snicker. "You do, too. You should see yourself."

We ran to the bathroom mirror to look at our purple selves. We stood there making crazy faces—laughing and making fun of each other. I was in heaven. Both of us had mothers with bad problems, but Madison was right. That didn't mean we couldn't be happy.

Grannie and Poppy's house sits in a forest on the edge of a beautiful marsh and river. My favorite place is the front porch in the early mornings where I can watch birds and deer and fiddler crabs starting their day. It's different each time and a great place to eat my cereal and think.

When I went out this morning, dark clouds hovered over the river, turning it navy blue. The sun peeped through in places like golden spotlights on the marsh, turning it different shades of green and brown. The wind whipping across the marsh grass looked like a hand petting a cat's fur. Deep booms of thunder rumbled and rattled in the distance. This storm meant business.

Grannie stepped out on the porch with a cup of coffee in her hand, sniffing the air. "Mystical morning, isn't it?"

"Uh'mmm, it is," I said. "I love it."

"Me, too. And I see my friend's here," she said, pointing to a large white bird hunched on a craggy piece of driftwood. "Sometimes he's there for hours at a time."

"He looks pretty pitiful and lonely to me."

She pulled up a rocking chair next to mine and said, "You know about being lonely, don't you, Love?"

"Lately, I do. Yeah. I try not to feel sorry for myself, but it's like I don't belong anywhere. Like I'm different from everyone else."

"Well, you're not," she said, setting her cup down in the saucer with a click. "You've got two arms, two legs, and a head on your shoulders—and a good one at that. We're proud of you."

"Oh, that's just because you're prejudiced, Grannie."

"Well, what's wrong with that?" she said with a laugh.

The whole sky instantly turned dark as the clouds swung closer and thunder drum-rolled around us.

"You don't suppose there's a tornado coming, do you, Grannie?'

"Goodness, no," she said. "Are you worried about that?"

"Not really—but this reminds me of that awful nightmare I have about the tornado tearing up our house and killing Mom. It's kind of scary, I guess."

Just then a blinding white, jagged bolt of lightening split the sky, causing both of us to jump like Jack-in-the-boxes in our seats. But the white bird calmly and deliberately lifted off from his perch, slowly flapping his wings and heading into the threatening sky as if he didn't have a care in the world.

"Look at him go, Grannie!" I said. "He's so brave. Not pitiful looking anymore, is he?"

"No. He understands the storm and how to survive it. And that's a good lesson for you. You're going to fly high, too, Darling. Just wait."

Chapter 17

*I'M LEARNING A LOT IN MS. CAROL'S group. Listening to some of the other kids makes me realize how lucky I am to have my family. At least I know I DO have a daddy and grandparents I can talk to about things if I want to. And for sure, I don't have to be afraid of them. But for some of the kids, our group is the only place they can feel safe. How horrible is that?

Skyler, the boy who Madison says usually misbehaves something awful, broke down and cried in front of all of us today. Big old tears were running down his face when he rolled up his shirtsleeve to show us what his father had done to him.

"See there," he said, pointing to four or five oozing red cigarette burns on the inside of his arm. "I should of known better than to get in his way when he was drunk."

Ms. Carol studied his burns, then tried to get him to look at her. "No, Skyler," she said, "remember we talked about every child having the right to expect a safe home? This isn't something you caused, Honey. Has it happened before?"

"Only if I don't watch out."

"Is this the first time you've told anyone?"

"Uh, huh," he said, rolling his sleeve back down over the raw places and carefully buttoning it around his wrist. "Cause I don't want to make trouble for him."

Ms. Carol propped both fists on her hips. "Look at me," she said. When Skyler finally did raise his eyes, she said, "Tell me. Do you think your father is likely to do this kind of thing to you again?"

"Probably, if he gets mad enough."

"Well, it sounds to me as if you need some help. Would you agree with that?"

"Maybe—I don't know."

"Listen," she said. "You have the right to ask for help. You and I'll talk some more about it after class, okay?"

She went back to her seat and said, "Okay, everybody. Who wants to go next?"

Tamara held up her hand and started talking about something that happened to her last week. But I wasn't actually listening. I was thinking about what Ms. Carol had said. You could tell she really believes kids have rights, too.

@

Things have been going good for me lately, even though Mom doesn't call me like she's promised—and when she does, I can tell she's been drinking. There's a certain way she slurs her words. It makes me sick to my stomach so I hang up on her. Madison says I should just tell her WHY. One of these days, I might do that. I wrote a letter to Mom like Ms. Carol suggested a long time ago telling her how it made me feel, but I never mailed it.

◎

Madison invited me for a sleep-over at her house last night, and it was a blast. We scrambled eggs and made milkshakes at midnight, and talked and talked and talked. She laughed when I told her I wanted to have a normal family.

"What's that?" she said. "If you snoop around, you'll find all families have problems of some kind."

"Well, I guess I just want to be a normal kid, then. Whatever that is."

She says for me to quit being a worry-wart.

"You need to lighten up and do things that make you happy," she said. "You'll make new friends. And they won't care about your mother."

"Sometimes I feel guilty, though, thinking about having fun and enjoying myself when I know Mom's so messed up."

"Oh, boy," she said, rinsing our dishes and stacking them in the sink. "I've heard that before." She turned and pointed her finger at me. "Listen, Emmy. Let me tell you something. You can't change your mother anymore than I can change mine."

@

Grannie and Poppy bought a special squishy foam mattress for me as a surprise. My bed is an antique that belonged to my great-grandparents. It's a four-poster that's so big I use a foot-stool to climb in it. Once I get on that mattress, I'm floating on a marshmallow cloud. Poppy calls my room the Princess Place since Grannie and I decorated it. I wanted it to look like a garden. So Aunt Bea, who's an artist, painted a white trellis on the green walls with lavender flowers spilling over it, and a window-box with red geraniums under one window. There's also a twisting yellow jessamine vine that grows up and over the tall, round-topped windows. She even added two rabbits, bees, butterflies, and a polka-dotted ladybug.

Sometimes I prop myself up in bed just so I can look at it and soak up every detail. Other times I read some of the books that help me understand more about Mom's problems. And lots of times I just lie there and think.

Madison said I need to do things that make me happy and I'll make new friends. I don't think looking at spit and snot and other stuff like bugs under Poppy's microscope is what she had in mind, but I love to do it, anyway. Maybe I'll be a biologist or even a mad scientist one day. Cool.

I love dancing, but I'm already taking lessons three times a week, so that takes care of that. Reading books and writing in my journal both make me happy, but those are things you do alone.

Madison says I ought to try out for the Panthers, the girl's basketball team. She says I'm tall, and they have lots of fun. Maybe. But I don't know. I've not played that much, except for shooting baskets at home with Daddy in the afternoons. He says I'm pretty good, actually.

After pondering all this stuff, I decided to make a list of goals for myself. They are:

1. *Make the Panthers team.*
2. *Make the Principal's List.*
3. *Don't feel sorry for myself.*
4. *Help somebody who's worse off than me.*

I added that last one because Grannie says that's the best way to stop feeling sorry for yourself. I like making lists because it makes me feel like I'm more in control of my life or something.

Poppy will be happy to hear that I'm setting goals. He believes you should set your mind to something and then do it. He also says every time I get a negative thought in my head, I need to replace it with a positive one. That's his favorite word.

So, besides the list of goals, I'm starting a list of all the good things in my life. That way, I'll have a positive thought ready whenever I need it.

As I waited in the locker room for Coach to give the okay for us to come out, my knees were knocking together like two Mexican maracas. Daddy had been working with me every day to prepare for this tryout. But scared as I was, how in the world would I run out there without tripping over my big feet and falling flat on my face in front of everybody?

Even though I'd succeeded in getting my hair into a slick ponytail that wouldn't fall into my eyes and blind me—and my gym shorts were long enough to not show my butt—and I had my lucky feather tucked in the bottom of my Reeboks—I still had the jitters.

Then a girl behind me gave me a little nudge. "Go on," she said, "Coach is calling us."

I quickly whispered a little prayer, "Oh, God, this is Emmy. Please help me do this."

From the minute I ran out onto the gym floor, something just came over me. I was a different person; like a moth out of a cocoon. I could hardly wait to show them that I was good enough to make the team. I was all over that floor, blocking throws and intercepting the ball. On top of that, I made three out of four free-throws.

We had to wait for what seemed like forever for the judging. I started getting all fluttery again, scared I didn't make it. Even though I'd practiced and practiced and practiced, maybe I just wasn't good enough. Then I remembered what Poppy said, and I began going over my list of positives.

All of a sudden, everybody stopped chattering as Coach motioned for quiet, then began calling off the numbers of those who made the team. "Number Three, Number Four, Number Seven—"

I couldn't breathe. She wasn't going to call my number.

"Number Nine, Number Ten, Number Twelve—"

Somebody punched me from behind. "Didn't you hear her call your number?" a voice said.

Then it hit me. Number Twelve. That was me! I was now a Panther. I'd actually *MADE IT!*

Chapter 18

MOM FINALLY CALLED AND SOUNDED straight, Daddy said. So he made arrangements to take me to meet her the next day for lunch at the Primrose Cafe. I fell asleep imagining the look on her face when I'd casually pull my Panther uniform out of my duffel bag and surprise her with my big news. She'd almost cry, she'd be so proud of me. I could hardly wait.

You know what happened? We drove up, and the first thing I see is Mom standing there in the parking lot wearing her big dark glasses, puffing on a cigarette, and looking like a walking stick. No joke.

"Mom, it's me!" I yelled, as soon as I could hop out of the car.

She whirled around with a big smile and held out her

twiggy arms to me, just like she used to do when I was little. Hugging her felt like hugging a bird, so that upset me. But it was her smell that made my stomach turn to stone.

"You stink like wine, Mom," I whispered. "I smell it."

"Oh, don't be silly, Emmy," she said, pulling away. "It's my perfume."

Daddy walked up just then and opened the door for us to go inside. I saw him look at Mom funny, but he didn't say anything. Until we got through ordering our food, that is.

He leaned back with his arms folded against his chest, shaking his head. "You've been hitting the bottle already this morning, haven't you, Susan?"

"You think I'm crazy?" she said, glaring at him. "I know better than to come around Emmy drunk."

"Oh, really?" he said. "It's never stopped you before."

Mom's hands were shaking as she started tearing off little pieces of her napkin in her lap.

She poked her head toward him like a turtle. "I'll have you know I haven't had a drink in six weeks, thanks to AA."

"So you are going to your AA group on a regular basis like the judge ordered, huh?" he said with a smirk.

"Every day," she said, her lips quivering.

"Well, that's very interesting, since I have a friend in that group and he says you've only been one time."

Mom's face turned red as a plum. I was starting to get a headache, and glad to see the waitress arrive with our food.

Nobody said anything while she was placing our plates on the table.

This might be a good time to change the subject, I thought. "Guess what, Mom?"

"What?" she said, not looking at me.

As the waitress walked away from our table, I reached into my duffel bag and whipped out my Panther uniform.

"Ta-Da! You're now sitting next to an official member of—"

"You don't know what you're talking about, Jack," Mom said. "I'll have you know that I'm going to a different AA group now."

"You've told that story too many times," he said, taking a sip of coffee.

I tugged on Mom's shirt sleeve.

"You're so smart, aren't you?" she said, still ignoring me. "You make me sick."

I tugged on her shirt again.

"Why don't you pay attention to your daughter, Susan?" he said. "She's been trying to tell you something."

"Oh, I'm sorry, Baby," she said, giving me a quick squeeze. "What were you saying?"

She was still cutting her eyes at Daddy, but I held the uniform up for her to see. "I made the Panthers, Mom. The basketball team."

She fingered it for a few seconds. "That's nice, Emmy. Nice material."

She turned and began clicking her fingernails on the table in front of Daddy. "Now, let me tell you one more thing, Mr.—"

I put my hand on her arm to stop her. I couldn't take anymore.

"Let's go, Daddy," I said, sliding out of the booth. "I need to. My head's hurting."

My heart was hurting, too, but how do you say that to your parents?

@

Madison and I agree that having an alcoholic parent makes you have to deal with stuff that shouldn't be part of growing up. I love Mom so much, but I don't know if I'll ever get over being mad at her.

@

Wow! Today was my first basketball game, and even though we didn't win, it was one of the best times of my life. I kept the bench warm until the last three minutes of the game. Then Coach motioned for me to go in. I glued my eyes on that ball so hard it felt like they were popping out of my head. It came flying right at the girl I was guarding, and I was ready. I sprang up like a kangaroo and intercepted the ball, then threw it right at Madison, who's the best forward on the team.

She charged down the court and we all blocked the other team just like we were supposed to. It was beautiful. But when she threw for the basket, it bounced off the rim.

So we lost the game, but it was still wonderful. All the other girls told me I did a real good job, especially for my first time. I love being part of a team. It makes you feel alive and really powerful.

@

Ms. Whittington had drawn a cute little smiley-face on my interim report sheet. She'd also written, "Keep up the good work, Emmy!"

She's probably been in shock that she hasn't had to get on me for day-dreaming lately.

Things have definitely been changing for me. And a lot of it is because of Madison. I would never have gone out for basketball if it hadn't been for her. And knowing what she's been through gave me the courage to do it. It just goes to show what a difference a good friend can make.

My list of positive things to remember is getting longer. Grannie calls it my "Blessings List".

@

Just when I'm finally beginning to feel better about myself—*WHAM!*

We were eating lunch in the cafeteria today when

Christi started passing out invitations to her birthday party. One-by-one, she handed a card to every girl at our table except me.

I waited—while everyone else opened their cards in a flurry of gossip and giggles—thinking that maybe she had more invitations in her backpack. That maybe she had just overlooked me.

When it was obvious she was through passing them out, I pasted a little smile on my face and said, "Where's your party going to be, Christi?" hoping to remind her that she hadn't given me a card even though I was sitting directly across from her.

She acted like she didn't hear me until Megan elbowed her and said, "Emmy's asking you a question, Christi."

"Adventure Park," she said without looking at me, then started waving and calling to someone at the next table. She might as well have added, "And you are not invited."

The burning shame I'd felt on the back of my neck shot up onto my scalp, spreading like a net. I sat with that silly smile frozen on my face and tried to blink away the tears stinging my eyes. What was the matter? Had I done something to make her mad?

Suddenly, the memory of that day long ago when Christi and I were in McDonald's with our moms came rushing back. Was that the problem? Or was it the time they saw her drunk at school? Or had her mother read the article in the paper about the DUI accident and decided for sure she didn't want Christi hanging around with me?

All those times I was trying to forget—would people always remember?

@

Grannie and I sat on the porch swing after I told her what happened at school, her arm snuggling me close like she used to do when I was little. Neither one of us said anything for a long time. We didn't need to. She knew how much it hurt, and I knew she would make it better if she could.

She's the best grandmother ever, but right now I miss my mom so much I can hardly stand it. It's kind of funny, really, because she's the one who caused me to have this problem with friends in the first place.

But girls need their mothers. That's why God made them. So they could be there when you hurt. So there would be somebody who loved you so much they'd die for you if they had to. Huh! That's a laugh. Mom wouldn't even give up wine for me.

I'm really angry at her. I really hate her. I really miss her.

Chapter 19

WHEN I OPENED THE FRONT DOOR, Madison grabbed me around the neck and hugged me so hard she just about knocked me over.

"She's coming home, Emmy! She's coming home!" she cried, jumping up and down.

"What? You don't mean it," I said. "You're talking about your—"

"Yes, my mother," she said, trying to catch her breath. "I ran all the way here to tell you. They gave her time off for good behavior, but she'll have to be on probation."

"What's that mean?"

"They'll be checking on her to make sure she doesn't go back to drinking and using drugs. If she does, she'll have to go back to prison for a long, long time."

"That's scary," I said.

"Yeah," she said, "it is kind of scary. Like I told you, at least I haven't had to worry about her while she's been in prison. But I can't think about that now. All I can think about is she's coming home. I'm going to have a mother again."

I was horrified to feel tears burn my eyes.

Madison noticed it immediately. "What's wrong, Emmy?"

"Oh, don't look at me," I said, feeling ashamed for thinking of myself. "I'm so happy for you—really I am—but I'm missing Mom so much. And I don't even like her right now. It's crazy."

Madison reached over and wiped the tears from my face with her fingers. "No, it's not. I haven't liked much about Mother for a long time. But I still love her just the same."

I couldn't help but grin. "You think that makes us both nuts?"

"Nope," she said. "That just makes us both normal."

@

Mother's Day is coming up. The special days bother me the most. All the times you're supposed to be together with your family. That's when I absolutely know she's gone.

Daddy took me to buy her a card, but I left without getting one. They all said things like, "My Wonderful Mother" or "World's Best Mom." How could I buy one like that? It gave me a headache to look at them.

I imagined other mothers in the world and what they would be doing on Mother's Day with their kids. I hated to think what mine would be doing.

In art class, we made beautiful little jewel boxes, covering them with maroon velvet and decorating them with different colored glass beads and ribbons. Some of the kids said they were going to give theirs to their mother and used silver beads to spell out Mom or Mama on the box.

Watching them made the hollow place around my heart get bigger. I didn't know whether I'd even see Mom for Mother's Day. The last three times she was supposed to meet me, she called at the last minute with some lame excuse why she couldn't come. I didn't believe any of them.

Why should I give her anything, anyway? She loves her wine more than she does me. Maybe I should give the box to Grannie. She's filling in as my mother, so maybe it wouldn't be fair to give it to Mom. But I'm not going to write Grannie's name on the jewel box just yet. I'll have to think about it.

@

Daddy and I were shooting baskets in the driveway when I heard the phone ringing. It was Mom. She sounded awful.

"What's wrong?" I said.

"I've been in the hospital and I miss my girl," she said, blubbering between every word.

"Why were you in the hospital? Are you okay?"

"No! I'm not, Baby," she said. "I'm sick, and Bob's lost his job—so he wants to move back to his hometown, and I—"

"Does that mean you're going with him?" I said, as my heart did a flip-flop.

She didn't answer at first, but I could hear the flick of her cigarette lighter and knew she'd be puffing away while we talked.

"I don't know what's going to happen," she said. Her voice sounded strange. "Put it this way. I can't live without Bob—but I can't live without my angel, either. You're going to have to come with me."

"I can't do that, Mom! You're not even supposed to be around me unless Daddy or Grannie is there. The judge said so. How would we go off somewhere and live together? That's crazy."

"Nobody would know where we were. We wouldn't let anybody know," she said, making a whistling noise as she blew out a long breath. I heard her take another puff on her cigarette. "I've got it all planned out."

"But I couldn't do that to Daddy or Grannie and Poppy. You know I—"

"Oh, is that right?" she said, her voice rising. "You mean you love them more than—"

"No! I don't love them more than you," I said. "But I can't just disappear and never see them again."

"But you could let ME move away—knowing you might not see me again—and here I am sick and needing you?" she said, almost in a screech.

"How sick ARE you, Mom?"

"You mean to tell me you'd choose your daddy and Grannie and Poppy over me?"

"I asked you—how sick ARE you?"

"Very—not that you care."

"I DO care, Mom—more than anything in the world. But I can't—"

"Oh! So you're choosing them over me, huh?" Her voice sounded flat; almost like a robot's. "That's the way it's going to be, huh?"

"Wait a minute," I said. "You've got the wrong—"
Click!

The sudden sound caught me by surprise. I couldn't believe it.

"Mom?" I said, pressing the phone hard against my ear. "Mom! Are you there?"

All I could hear was a humming dial tone. My fingers shook as I punched in her phone number. It rang and rang and rang. I pictured her sitting by the phone, refusing to answer. It continued to ring and ring and ring—the loneliest sound in the world.

Suddenly, I remembered Thomas from my group telling

us about how his mother tried to commit suicide by taking an overdose of sleeping pills. Maybe that's what Mom was doing. Maybe right this very moment she was swallowing the pills! My mind shifted to an image of her sprawled out on the bed—dying from an overdose of something—feeling alone and unloved by her one and only child—me.

Me! How would I feel if she killed herself because of me? Was it wrong to tell her I couldn't go with her? Maybe Bob wasn't nice like she said and was actually mean to her. Was I supposed to be taking care of her since she always said I was her angel?

So I got down on my knees and prayed, Dear God, this is me again. Emmy. I've got big trouble this time. Please show me what to do.

I waited, but didn't hear any booming voice from heaven or anything like that. But an idea did finally pop into my head. My heart frammed and frammed against my chest as I picked up the phone and dialed 911.

Daddy sprang from the kitchen table at the first ring of the doorbell and beat me to the front door.

"Come on in, Sir," Daddy said, waving the deputy inside. He was a huge man, filling the foyer with his dark-green uniform. The leather belt and gun holster around his too-fat waist made a crunching sound as he moved into the living room. I followed right behind him.

"My mom's dead, isn't she?" I said to his back.

He spun around so fast I bumped smack against him. "Oh, no, little lady," he said, grabbing my arm to steady me. "She's not dead—just very, very drunk."

She was alive! I was so relieved my bones instantly felt like they'd turned to rubber. Daddy must have sensed I felt weak because he made me sit down. I peered up at the deputy's worn-looking face. "Sir, you're sure my mom's going to be all right?"

He cleared his throat, studying me. "She's okay for now," he said. He stood there for a minute as if he didn't know what else to say. Or maybe he was looking right into my heart. "Your mom's been giving you a rough time lately, hasn't she?" he said in a soft voice.

That did it! To my total humiliation, right there in front of that nice man, the tears and the anger I'd been holding back forever just broke loose. "How did you know?" I wailed between sobs, grabbing the box of tissue Daddy held out to me. "How'd you know?"

"I see the signs," he said. "And I've been there myself."

I couldn't believe what he was telling me. I blew my nose one more time and said, "YOU were an alcoholic?"

He and Daddy exchanged glances, then he chuckled and said, "No, young lady. My DAD was the alcoholic. What I'm saying is, I've walked in your shoes. I can't tell you how many times the police had to come to our house. Either because Dad was threatening me or my mother, or because he was passed out and we couldn't wake him up. I know what it's like to worry constantly. To live with the shadow of your parent's sorry life hanging over your head."

He hesitated for a moment, then pulled up a chair and sat directly in front of me so we were eyeball to eyeball.

"Listen, Sweetie," he said. "I can tell you're a sharp girl. You know your mom's got problems, right? The truth is— this may not be the last time you have a scare."

"But what can I do, then?"

"Remember you're just a kid." He leaned over and gave me a fake punch on the arm. "Your mom's actually trapped by her addiction, okay? It keeps her from having a better life. But you're not trapped. Your whole life is ahead of you. Get ready."

@

After I took my bath, Daddy came in to kiss me good-night. I hugged him extra-hard. Raisin curled up into a U-shape at the foot of my bed, and as usual I reached for old Dolly to snuggle with.

Daddy had a little grin on his face. "Tell me, what are you going to do when you're engaged to be married and your fiance says you can't take your rag doll on your honeymoon?"

"That's easy," I said. "Not get married."

"You're such a romantic," he said, laughing as he closed the door.

I lay there thinking about when I was a happy, dumb little kid with no worries, carrying Dolly everywhere with me. It was kind of funny that she was still so important to me. The first time Madison spent the night with me and saw Dolly, she admitted that she still slept with her stuffed bear, BoBo. We laughed about it—calling each other big babies.

But maybe we are, sometimes. Maybe we hang on to these things because we're not actually ready to be all grown up yet—or be responsible for somebody else.

Yeah. It's like I told Madison about some of the problems we heard from other friends in our group. When a parent is an alcoholic, lots of times the parent becomes the kid, and the kid becomes the parent. That's what's been going on with Mom and me, I know.

A full moon shone through my big bedroom window, making everything look dream-like. I lay there in the soft light, getting sleepy, and pulled Dolly close to me. Like when I was a little girl. It felt good.

Chapter 20

THE MAROON VELVET JEWEL BOX sat on my desk, still unfinished. I couldn't make up my mind about whose name to put on it. Mom and I hadn't talked since I called 911 on her, but Grannie had made arrangements for us to meet her for a picnic in the park for Mother's Day.

I still didn't have a gift for Mom, and I knew she'd love the jewel box. But I felt guilty giving it to her because she wasn't the one taking care of me anymore. So that probably meant I needed to give it to Grannie.

Just as I was reaching for the silver beads and the glue to write her name on the box, Grannie came up behind me, scaring me almost out of my skin.

"Goodness! I'm sorry—I didn't mean to sneak up on you," she said, with a laugh. Then she spied the box. "How precious! You must have made that for your mother."

I didn't know what to say. Should I tell her how confused I was about the whole thing? That would probably hurt her feelings, though.

"Actually, Grannie," I finally said, acting as if I saw something incredibly interesting on the carpet, "it's not for Mom. It's for you."

"Hey! This is me—your grannie," she said, tilting my chin up so I had to look at her. "Do I sense a little misplaced guilt here?"

"What do you mean?"

"I suspect you've been tormenting yourself needlessly," she said. "You don't ever have to feel guilty about loving your mom, Honey. You're not being disloyal to me. I don't expect you to replace her with me in your affection. She's still your mother to love with all your heart—and always will be. That doesn't take anything away from me."

"Oh, Grannie, you're super," I said, and hugged her so hard she had to beg me to stop so she could breathe.

"Let me out of here so you can finish that and get dressed," she said. "It's almost time for your dance lesson."

Using a glue bottle and silver beads, I made a heart on the lid of the box. Then right in the middle, I put the word "MOM", because like Grannie said, she'd always be there.

That's one of the reasons I like doing art so much. You can express your deep-inside feelings, kind of like writing in your journal. It was easy for me to draw a heart and show her the love that's there for her. That's the good stuff.

But there's other stuff in my heart, too. All the jumbled-up feelings that won't go away and make it so heavy. I wished I could gather up all the hurt and tears and shame in one bundle to give to her so she'd understand. Maybe it would help her to stop forever.

Then suddenly, it came to me.

It was just a little slip of paper that I carefully folded up before placing in the box. But it said everything I carried in my heart.

Mom, how could you choose wine over me?

I love you always, Emmy.

Quickly, before I could change my mind, I closed the lid, then wrapped my gift in beautiful silvery paper and scotch-taped it closed.

@

After basketball practice, Madison took me home with her to meet her mother. I couldn't imagine what somebody who'd been in jail would be like, so I was a little bit nervous. She turned out to be a really nice lady. I guess because she smoked cigarettes, she had quite a few wrinkles on her face, but she was still pretty. Madison went to the kitchen to fix us all some lemonade, and her mother and I sat together on the back deck.

"Emmy, I want to thank you for being such a good friend to Madison," she said with a smile.

"Oh, she's the one who's been good to me," I said, surprised.

"Well, I'm glad to hear that. But she tells me you're her very special friend. You know—the kind everybody needs. Someone she could open up to and share her deepest feelings."

She looked suddenly tired. "You and I both know, Emmy, that I've hurt her deeply. I can never replace this time that we've lost. But I've promised her that with God's help I'll never go back to what I was."

Before I even thought, I said, "You really think so?" My face turned hot. I was totally embarrassed at myself!

The quick twinkle in her eye reminded me of Madison. "I know it's hard to believe after what you've heard about my past history," she said, smiling again, "but I'm going to give it my best. The good news is that even though there's no cure for alcoholism, people can recover. It's up to them—and in my case, it's up to me."

"I don't think my mother wants to get well," I said.

"Sometimes it takes a big jolt of reality to break the hold it can have on you. I look back at the things I've done and I can hardly—"

Just then, the back door slammed as Madison came out carrying lemonade and cookies on a tray. She stopped and gave her mother a little kiss on top of her head, then set the tray down on the table. They smiled at each other like they'd just discovered the most wonderful secret in the world.

It made me feel good to see them, and I felt better about myself for that. Being jealous like I was before—because Madison was going to have her mother back—just made me miserable inside. Like Poppy says, if you want to *HAVE* a good friend, you need to *BE* a good friend.

◎

I dreamed about Mom again last night. At first, it was good. I was a teeny little kid again, and we were playing under the sprinkler in our bathing suits. She chased me, and we were both squealing and giggling like crazy. When she caught me, she picked me up and swung me around until I was so dizzy I could hardly stand up. I wobbled like a top all over the yard.

Then I fell hard, face-down on the driveway and cut my lip. I screamed bloody-murder, and before you could say Jack Sprat she was there, grabbing me up in her arms and holding me tight. I can still feel it even this morning, with her kisses all over my face. That's the way she was before the drinking—so wonderful and loving and worried about me and everything.

But then the dream turned into my scary tornado nightmare again. As always, Daddy and I saw it thundering our way.

"Susan, look what's coming towards us!" he yelled, motioning frantically. "We've got to get out of here."

She just stood there drinking a glass of wine as if she didn't hear him.

For the first time in the dream, I yanked the drink out of her hand and threw it as hard as I could. The glass hit the wall and shattered into a million pieces. The wind swirled all around us, and trees started sailing through the air. Windows were breaking all over the house.

"Come on, Mom, please!" I cried, pulling on her arm. "Don't you see what's happening? *PLEASE!*"

But she paid no attention to me. It was as if she didn't even see me anymore. I began sobbing as the house started flying apart and she wouldn't move.

Daddy grabbed my other hand and snatched me away. "Run, Emmy, run!" he screamed. "You can't save your mom—you've got to save yourself!"

Everything went black, and I heard somebody wailing and wailing and wailing. The sound woke me up, and I realized it was me.

Chapter 21

J SAT IN THE BACK SEAT OF Grannie's car and prayed over and over all the way to the playground. "Dear God," I said, "this is me again. Please make Mom be sober for Mother's Day. And please don't let my note hurt her feelings."

Grannie and I were the first ones there, so we picked out a picnic table that was in a shady spot by the merry-go-round. She unfolded the plastic tablecloth and covered the table with it. I helped her set out the food and drinks and other stuff.

Then I placed my gift to Mom right smack in the middle of the table.

"You did a beautiful job of wrapping your mom's gift," Grannie said. "I know she's going to love it."

"I sure hope so," I said. "I put something in it that I don't—"

"Oh, here she comes," Grannie said, waving to Mom. "Go meet her."

We met at the swings and hugged each other really hard while little kids yelled all around us. She was wearing a really stinky perfume. But it didn't cover up the smell of whatever she'd been drinking. I just hoped Grannie wouldn't notice and make us leave. She won't let Mom get near me if she's drinking and would snatch me away from there in a heartbeat. She can really be tough if she wants to.

"Let me look at you," Mom said, holding my shoulders and squinting at me. Her eyes were puffy and bloodshot, as if she'd been crying. She gave me a quick kiss on the cheek. "You're growing up too fast. Where did my little girl go?"

"Right here," I said, feeling sad and glad all at the same time. It made me happy to see her, but she'd lost so much weight it looked as if she'd put on somebody else's clothes by mistake. And it hurt to know she had to take a drink before coming to see me.

We walked up to the picnic table and Mom said hello to Grannie, who was sitting there reading a book. Then she held out a blue gift bag to me. "Here, Emmy," she said, "these are a few little things I picked up for you."

"But it's your Mother's Day," I said, peeking into the bag. "You're not supposed to be giving me gifts."

"Don't be silly," she said. "Go ahead and look."

She had bought me all kinds of stuff for my hair—scrunchies, hairclips, hairbands, and ponytail holders. I lined them up all in a row on the table, then took three pairs of ankle socks with wild polka-dots and striped designs out of the bag.

"Wow—these are really cool," I said, glancing at Mom. She had a big grin on her face.

I reached back into the bag and felt something hard wrapped in yellow tissue paper.

"Oh, how adorable!" I said, gazing at the little porcelain angel with pink-tipped wings that fit in the palm of my hand.

"I knew you'd love it. I thought of you right away when I saw it."

"That's a very sweet keepsake, Susan," Grannie said.

She began taking sandwiches and fruit out of the cooler. "If you're as hungry as I am," she said, "we can go ahead and eat. Then I think I'll take my folding chair over there in the sun to get some Vitamin D and read my book. That'll give you two a chance to visit."

After Grannie moved her chair to the other side of the swing sets, Mom and I finished cleaning off the table. The only thing left was the velvet jewel box wrapped in silvery paper.

"Is this for me?" Mom said with a little smile.

I swallowed hard around the lump in my throat. "Uh-huh—it's for Mother's Day," I said, which was a dumb thing to say because of course she already knew that.

She had a hard time unwrapping it because her fingers were trembling so bad. "I hate to tear this paper," she said. "It's too nice."

Finally, she saw the jewel box. "Oh, this is gorgeous!" she said with a little squeal, wearing a beauty queen smile. She picked it up and turned it over and over, examining my designs. "No one has ever given me anything so beautiful."

"Gee, thanks," I said. I don't think I was breathing as she turned the tiny latch to open the lid. I was too busy praying.

She lifted the lid and saw the little note. "Well, what's this?" she said, as if she'd just found pirate gold.

She looked so happy, I thought about snatching the note out of her hand and throwing it in the trashcan.

But she'd already unfolded it and began reading out loud.

"How could you choose wine over me, Mom?

I love you always, Emmy"

Then she read it a second time to herself, eyebrows scrunched tight, lip-syncing the words.

All I can tell you is that at first she looked like she was struggling with all her might to hold her face together. She took a deep breath and slowly folded the paper just the way it was and closed the lid without looking at me. Then she crumpled.

We both were crying.

"Oh, Baby, how could you think that?"

"Because that's what you did," I said, grabbing a napkin to blow my nose. I handed one to her. "You chose wine over me."

"No," she said, shaking her head. "The reason I have to drink is because your grandmother took you away from me."

"Uh-uhh—you know that's not true, Mom. The judge gave you a choice, remember?"

Her eyes glinted. "Your grannie told you to say that, didn't she?"

"No. I'm not stupid. I know what happened."

She looked down and picked at her fingernails for what seemed a long time without saying anything. She looked like a little kid, pouting.

Finally, she said, "If you'd come live with me, I could probably stop."

"That wouldn't make any difference, Mom. I can't make you stop."

Her lips quivered as she held up her finger to me for our Best Friends Promise. "But you're my best friend. I need you."

I reached out and clutched her finger in my fist. "Mom, I'm your kid—not your best friend. And I need you, too.

But I need you to be my mom. And you can't be as long as you're drinking. Don't you see that?"

For a minute she looked puzzled, as if what I was saying didn't make any sense to her at all. Then a look of horror passed over her face and she covered her eyes with both hands.

"Oh, Dear God," she cried, "what have I done to my baby? What have I done?"

It made my heart split right in two. I moved around to her side of the table and wrapped my arms around her. She leaned against me and bawled and bawled and bawled.

"I'm so sorry, Baby," she said, crying so hard she was barely able to say the words. "I'm so sorry. I never meant to—"

"It's okay, Mom. I know you're sick. You need to get well."

"But I can't," she said, shaking her head. "I tried and it's no use. I'm just like my daddy. He drank until the day he died."

"That doesn't mean you have to. It's a choice, Mom. Don't you know that?"

She suddenly sat up straight and grabbed a napkin to blow her nose. "You don't understand, Emmy. Nothing—"

"Mom, listen to me," I said, knocking on the table to get her attention. "You don't have to give up. Alcoholics CAN get better. They CAN recover."

She narrowed her eyes, looking at me as if she hardly

recognized me. "You've changed," she said.

"Maybe a little. I learned some things."

"Like what?"

"I don't want to hurt your feelings."

"No, go ahead," she said. "Tell me."

"That I can't control what you do, so I can't make your problems go away. It may sound mean, but I've had to learn that I can't let the way you live ruin my life. Even if you keep drinking, I can still turn out to be a good person and a happy person."

"Ouch! I felt that," she said, hunching her shoulders as if I'd hit her. "Where did that come from? Your daddy?"

"My counselor, actually—and lots of other people."

She began twisting the napkin into a tight roll. "What did you do? Run around telling everybody what a terrible mother I am?"

"Oh, Mom, if you only knew how hard I tried to keep everything a secret. I didn't want anybody to know. But they did, anyway—at school, at dancing, at church. I was so ashamed, I could have just died."

"Then what?"

"My counselor, Ms. Carol, taught me that it wasn't my fault what you were doing. And she said trying to keep everything a deep secret—and all my feelings shut up in-side—was the worst thing I could do. She says the poison builds up inside, kind of like a boil. And that you can't heal until you lance the wound. You know. Get rid of all the bad stuff."

"I wish there had been a Ms. Carol in my life back when I was your age. Things might have been different." Her nose was dripping, but she didn't seem to notice or care. She just kept twisting the napkin, tighter and tighter.

"It's not too late, Mom," I said, grabbing a clean one and wiping her nose for her. "My best friend, Madison— her mother was probably worse than you. And she's doing really good now. She says she'll help you if you want. You can go to Alcoholics Anonymous together."

"It never helped before," she said, shaking her head.

"She gave me her name and phone number to give you. Said to give her a call. She's very nice—honest."

I took the card from my purse and held it out to her. "Here—you want it?"

She looked at it as if it might bite her. "I don't know. Why would she want to help me?"

"That's what it's all about, Mom. I've learned that. You help yourself when you help somebody else."

I offered the card to her again. "Come on, Mom, do it," I said. "For you—and for me."

She looked down at the table for the longest time without moving. Finally, she reached for the card.

"I'm not making any promises," she said. "I've broken enough already."

I squeezed her hand and kissed her on the cheek. "I know, Mom," I said, "I know."

Chapter 22

J COULDN'T SLEEP TONIGHT THINKING about my get-together with Mom on Mother's Day. What I said to her about the stuff I'd learned was true. Once I decided to let them, a lot of people helped me. Maybe one of these days I'll write a book and tell my story to help other kids know they're not alone.

Anyway, there's no telling whether what I said to Mom will do any good or not, but I feel so much better after being honest with her. Kind of like, I'm free. It's up to her, now. I don't know why I keep asking God to make Mom do anything. I used to think he could boss us around—and of course he could if he wanted to—but he doesn't. We have a choice.

That's what Mom needs to understand. Even though

she has a disease, she can still choose not to drink because it makes her even more sick. So I just need to remember to pray that she'll make good choices.

And me, too.

⊚

Today was the last game of the season for the Panthers. Coach had been drilling us and drilling us on the importance of teamwork. And Daddy believes in being prepared. So every afternoon, he and I have been practicing.

I've been getting good with my hoop shots—very few air balls. Lots of times, I beat Daddy, and he used to be a great basketball player.

When I tease him about it, he says it's like life. You're not always going to win. But you just prepare yourself for the next game and keep trying. Most of all, he says, play for the joy of it.

When we got to the gymnasium, the parking lot was already getting full. This was going to be a big game. My stomach started getting fluttery.

The noise in the locker room would bust your eardrums. Girls can be loud!

"Hey, Emmy!" I heard somebody shout. It was Madison waving at me.

I plopped my gymbag down on the bench next to her. "You beat me here. I can't believe it."

"I've been dying to tell you something," she said, "so I got here early."

"Why didn't you just call me?"

"I wanted to see your face," she said, shaking her fists with excitement. "Guess what? Guess what?"

"What?"

"Your mom finally called my mom! They're going to an AA meeting together tomorrow night!"

We grabbed each other and squealed and squealed and squealed, jumping up and down like we were on pogo sticks. We made so much racket, everybody in the locker room stopped talking all at once. They thought we'd gone bonkers or something.

Suddenly, Coach was there, telling us to hustle and do our very best. She began calling out names of the starters. When I heard Madison's name and then mine, it was like a little electric jolt went through my whole body.

The gym was packed full, and everybody was standing up, cheering for us as we trotted in. I didn't have time to look in the crowd for all the people who told me they'd be there, rooting for me. But I knew they were there. My heart filled my whole chest.

The whistle blew, and we took our positions, waiting for the tip-off. I looked over at Madison, and she was looking at me with a big grin. I gave her a thumbs-up.

We were winners, and we were ready.

The End

...and the beginning, too!

You

are not

alone !

B. Acosta

Resources

If you need help or just somebody to talk to, you can call these FREE hotlines. Be sure and dial the number 1 first.

CHILDHELP USA Child Abuse Hotline: 1-800-422-4453

Girls and Boys Town National Hotline: 1-800-448-3000

Youth Crisis Hotline: 1-800-448-4663

Many other organizations can help, too, especially by providing information on the Internet. The more you learn about alcoholism, the better. Remember, knowledge is power! Here are their Internet website addresses and phone numbers. If you don't have a computer at home, go to your library and a librarian will help you.

Alateen
1-888-425-2666
www.alateen.org
A fellowship of young Al-Anon members whose lives have been affected by someone else's drinking.

Betty Ford Center Children's Program
1-800-854-9211
www.bettyfordcenter.org
Website provides resources for children of alcoholics and addicts. Children's program offers intensive prevention and education groups for children whose lives have been impacted by a loved ones' addiction to alcohol or other drugs.

Free Vibe
www.freevibe.com
Here, kids share their experiences and learn how to resist peer pressure and make good choices for the future.

Girl Power (sponsored by the U.S. Dept. of Health & Human Services)

www.girlpower.gov/

Helps to encourage and empower 9-14 year old girls to make the most of their lives. Has a great section for children of alcoholics: Click on "You're Not Alone".

National Association for Children of Alcoholics

1-888-554-2627

www.nacoa.org/kidspage

A national nonprofit organization working to help children of alcohol and drug dependent parents.

Their website has a special link for kids as well as important information for parents.

The Children's Place

650-216-7211

www.thechildrensplaceprogram.org

Provides a summer camp retreat and other educational programs for children of alcoholics designed to end the cycle of addiction.

Excellent website for kids and parents.

Books

If you'd like to read more about children of alcoholics, take this list to the library and your librarian can help you. Or an adult may order a book for you.

Alateen—A Day At a Time. Virginia Beach, VA, Al-Anon Family Group Headquarters, Inc. Offers a thought for every day.

Alateen—Hope for Children of Alcoholics. Al-Anon Family Group Headquarters, Inc. 1980. Explains what Al-Anon is all about.

Daddy Doesn't Have to be a Giant Anymore. Clarion Books. New York, NY. 1996. (out of print, but may be in libraries)

Dear Kids of Alcoholics. Lindsey Hall & Leigh Cohn. Gurze Designs & Books. 1988.

Kid's Power Too!: Words to Grow By. Cathey Brown, Betty LaPorte and Jerry Moe. Imagin Works. Dallas, TX. 1996. Offers a thought for every day.

Kit for Kids, booklet by the National Association for Children of Alcoholics, available at www.nacoa.org.

Living Today in Alateen. Virginia Beach, VA: Al-Anon Family Group Headquarters, inc. 2001. A collection of personal sharings from Alateen members around the world. There is a different page for each day of the year.

My Dad Loves Me, My Dad Has a Disease. Claudia Black. Mac Publishing. Third edition. 2000. Bainbridge Island, WA. A workbook that helps young people learn about themselves, their feelings, and the disease of addiction in their families through art therapy. Children between the ages of 6 and 14 share what it is like for them to live in a family with alcoholism or drug addiction.

When a Family Is In Trouble. Children Can Cope Series. Marge Heegard. Woodland Press. Minneapolis, MN. 1991.

For the Grownups

Adult Children of Alcoholics (ACoA)
310-534-1815
www.adultchildren.org
Posts meeting lists and resources.

Al-Anon Information Services
888-425-2666

www.al-anon.alateen.org
Posts meeting lists and maps to area Al-Anon, Alateen, and Pre-teen meetings. All information available in Spanish.

Alcoholics Anonymous (AA)
Look in your local phone book for number.
www.alcoholics-anonymous.org
Provides information about AA and gives contact information for local meetings.

Narcotics Anonymous
888-629-6757
www.na.org
Provides literature and info on recovery and local meetings.

Resources Information For Children Of Alcoholics

Self-Help Groups

Al-Anon Family Group Headquarters, Inc.
1600 Corporate Landing Parkway
Virginia Beach, VA 23454-5617
1-888-4AL-ANON
www.al-anon.org

Alcoholics Anonymous (get info)

Alateen
1-800-344-2666 (for meeting information)
1-800-356-9996 (literature)
Both numbers: 8:00 a.m.-6:00 p.m. (EST) M-F
www.alateen.org/alateen.html

Adult Children of Alcoholics (ACA/ACoA)
P.O. Box 3216
Torrance, CA 90510
(310)534-1815
www.adultchildren.org

Girl Power (??) look up
www. girlpower.gov/girlarea/notalone/resources.htm

National Associations

American Academy of Child and Adolescent Psychiatry (AACAP)
(800)333-7636, ext. 131
www.aacap.org

Mothers Against Drunk Driving (MADD)

National Association for Children of Alcoholics (NACoA)
11426 Rockville Pike, Suite 100
Rockville, MD 20852
(888)554-COAS (2627)
www.nacoa.org/kidspage.htm
ncadi.samhsa.gov/nacoa/
nacoa@erols.com

National Association for Native American Children of Alcoholics (NANACoA)
130 Andover Park East, Suite 210
Seattle, WA 98188
(800)322-5601

National Black Alcoholism Council (NBAC)
1629 K Street NW, Suite 802
Washington, DC 20006
(202)296-2696

National Council on Alcoholism and Drug Dependence (NCADD)
12 West 21st Street, 7th Floor
New York, NY 10017
(800)NCA-CALL
www.ncadd.org

Alchohol & Drug Prevention Information

Children of Alcoholics Foundation
164 West 74th Street
New York, NY 10023
(212)595-5810 ext. 7760
Fax (212) 595-2553
www.coaf.org

National Clearinghouse for Alcohol and Drug Information (NCADI)
P.O. Box 2345
Rockville, MD 20847-2345
(800) 729-6686
ncadi.samhsa.gov

National Institute on Alcohol Abuse and Alcoholism (NIAAA)
5635 Fishers Lane, MSC 9304
Bethesda, Maryland 20892-9304
www.niaaa.nih.gov/
(updated website for middle schoolers)

Hotlines

ChildHelp USA Child Abuse Hotline
1/800/422-4453

National Youth Crisis Hotline
1-800-448-4663

National Runaway Switchboard
1-800-621-4000

About The Author

Jeannine Auth is a native of St. Augustine, Florida. She and her husband, Dennis, live on a barrier island wedged between the Atlantic Ocean and the Intracoastal Waterway—a magnet for nieces, nephews, grandchildren, and other intriguing creatures. She's a former environmental lobbyist, public speaker, and non-profit association director with a life-long passion for books and writing.

Things To Think About
And Other Notes To Myself

*Things To Think About
And Other Notes To Myself*

Things To Think About
And Other Notes To Myself

Things To Think About
And Other Notes To Myself

Things To Think About
And Other Notes To Myself

Quick Order Form

To place your order:

Visit our website: www.morningtidepress.com

E-mail: morningtide@bellsouth.net

Fax: 904/823-9978 Send this form

Call toll free: 877-823-9978   Have a credit card ready

Mail orders: Morningtide Press

P.O. Box 312

St. Augustine, FL 32085-0312

Shipping by air:

Quantity:_____@$16.99 each   _____

US: $4 for first book   _____

$2 for each additional book   _____

Tax: FL residents add 6%: $1.02   _____

Total: _____

Shipping information:

Name:_____

Address: _____

_____

City: _____State____Zip_____

Please have the author autograph the book as follows:

_____

Payment:

___Check or money order   ___Credit Card

Please circle: Visa   MasterCard   Discover

Card number: _____

Name on card: _____

Expiration date: _____

Thank You!